Beyond Borders

The Wyndham Place Trust was founded in 1959 to promote among men and women of religious faith a concern for peace, world order and the rule of law. For this purpose it brings together a range of people of various vocations and specializations and those associated with a wide range of political and religious opinions.

As its contribution towards achieving this goal, and a world at peace, the Trust undertakes research and educational activities. It seeks to enlighten public opinion and arouse concern about problems that must be faced in fashioning a world society in an age of interdependence.

Beyond Borders

West European Migration
Policy Towards the
21st Century

SARAH COLLINSON

Royal Institute of International Affairs

Wyndham Place Trust

First published in Great Britain in 1993 by
the Royal Institute of International Affairs
Chatham House, 10 St James's Square, London SW1Y 4LE

Distributed by The Brookings Institution, 1775 Massachusetts Avenue
Northwest, Washington DC 20036-2188, USA

British Library Cataloguing in Publication Data

A CIP catalogue record for this book is available from
the British Library

ISBN 0 905031 71 7

Text designed and set by Hannah Doe
Cover design by Youngs Design in Production
Printed and bound in Great Britain by Redwood Books

Contents

Foreword

In 1992 the Council of the Wyndham Place Trust decided to initiate
a study of emerging trends in the field of migration into Western
Europe. The dismantling of the 'iron curtain' in 1989 had created
a wholly new situation. The constraints of the Cold War fell away
and the citizens of large parts of Europe began to feel free to move
from their homes if they thought this necessary or desirable. Fears
were expressed in Western Europe that substantial immigration
from Central and Eastern Europe would be added to the immigration from the Southern and Eastern Mediterranean countries and
other parts of the world. In addition to new economically motivated migration from Central and Eastern Europe, the conflict in
the ex-Yugoslav countries has added a large volume of emigration
of populations fleeing from violence, expulsion and expropriation,
particularly in Bosnia.

The Wyndham Place Trust is concerned that immigrant pressures can give rise to serious social and political difficulties unless
two conditions can be met. Coherent migration policies need to be
agreed by West European countries; and their citizens have to be
helped to understand the issues at stake and to deal positively with
the impact of immigration on their own lives and that of their
localities. The Trust was thus interested to produce a report which
would provide information on migration in a way that might be
helpful to policy-makers and the public alike.

The Royal Institute of International Affairs now has an established programme of research into international migration and
migration policy headed by Sarah Collinson, who has been based

at the Institute as a Research Fellow since April 1991. This publication follows on from Sarah Collinson's book *Europe and International Migration* (Pinter Publishers for RIIA, 1993), which concentrates on the historical, political and geographical background to current developments in the policy field. We feel particularly pleased to have secured Ms Collinson as the author of this report, and are very grateful for the accomplished way in which she has undertaken this study.

The centrepiece of the project was the Institute's second international workshop on migration policy, which was convened in November 1992. Both the Wyndham Place Trust and the RIIA are indebted to the academics, policy-makers and practitioners who took part for providing an important sounding-board for some of the issues and ideas included in the study.

We would also like to thank the other members of the project Steering Committee, which was composed of representatives of the RIIA: Dr Philip Robins (Head of the Middle East Programme), and Professor J.S. Spence (Director of Studies); and representatives of the Wyndham Place Trust, acting in their personal capacities: Dr Martyn Bond (Head of the UK Office of the European Parliament, member of the WPT Council), Lieut. Cdr Roland Hudson DSO DFC (formerly of the Conference of British Missionary Societies, member of the WPT Council), Charles Regan (formerly Under Secretary, DHSS, member of the WPT Council), A. Bryan Saunders (formerly Assistant Secretary, Department of Transport, lately Chairman of Brighton Council of Voluntary Service, Treasurer of the WPT), Mrs Fiona Shipley (Executive Secretary of the WPT), Mr Michael Smart (formerly Head of the European Communities Branch, Dept of Employment, Chairman of European Dialogue, member of the WPT Council), Mrs Muriel Smith MBE (formerly Adviser on Community Work, Home Office, member of the WPT Council), and Professor George Wedell FRTS (lately Director-General of the European Institute for the Media, Chairman of the WPT). Their advice and counsel throughout the duration of the project was invaluable. Mrs Fiona Shipley deserves a special mention for ensuring close liaison between the Institute and the Wyndham Place Trust.

Of course, without financial support from the Le Poer Power Trust, the Joseph Rowntree Charitable Trust, and the Beatrice Hankey Foundation, the project could not have gone ahead. We are therefore especially grateful to our sponsors for their generous support.

This study addresses the current public policy debate at both national and European levels. Chapter 1 examines the real or perceived threats posed by migration in Western Europe today. Chapter 2 considers the question of immigrant integration, and questions whether the countries of Western Europe are yet reconciled to the presence of substantial immigrant minority populations. Chapter 3 considers Europe's immigration controls, focusing on the factors which constrain the implementation of an effective system of enforcement. Chapter 4 looks at the current state of refugee policy in Western Europe, and questions how well equipped it is to deal with the challenges posed by rising numbers of asylum-seekers and new large-scale population displacements in some parts of the European continent.

Owing to the complexity of the issues, the alternatives to current forms of management and control are by no means clear. Chapter 5 aims to provide pointers as to how some of the shortcomings of today's migration and refugee policies could be overcome. It is questioned how, in the short term, policy-makers might move beyond defensive reactions and begin to shift the policy debate in a more constructive direction. In this context, Chapter 5 considers the question of transparency in policy-making, and the potential for supporting particular categories of migration. Looking to the longer term, it is argued that only when policy-makers recognize the reality of migration as a continuing process will more effective, realistic and sustainable policies begin to be developed.

It is clear that migration, which has been a feature of European society throughout history, will continue. Thus efforts to achieve policies which deal with migration in a humane and politically responsible manner will depend both on government action and public support. Burden-sharing between states should become the rule. States should make a positive commitment to the challenges and opportunities that flow from the erosion of barriers to free movement since 1989. In the area of public support, the churches, other religious bodies and non-governmental organizations have an important role to play.

Many of the fears which influence politicians and their constituents about the arrival of large numbers of immigrants have little basis in fact. In a world in which millions of people are being forced to move as a consequence of war, deprivation and natural disasters, the idea of unmanageable immigration easily evokes panic. But it is not clear that Britain or the rest of Western Europe as a whole appears at present to be threatened with an overwhelming mass inflow of migrants. The Federal Republic of Germany has had, it is true, a special problem arising from its extensive land frontiers and the constitutional provisions regarding asylum. But there is no reason to believe that, with the sympathetic support of its neighbours, this problem cannot be solved. Again, the Mediterranean countries of Europe have a problem in dealing with migratory pressures (both legal and illegal) from the Maghreb countries and the Middle East. The numbers involved are not, however, such as to constitute an overarching threat to those countries. At the time of writing it is impossible to forecast how the conflict in Bosnia will end. However, the possibility of large numbers of Bosnian refugees requiring resettlement cannot be discounted.

These exceptional situations reinforce the recommendations of this report, especially for more open policy-making and better public information about the measures necessary to implement them with humanity and efficiency. Thus we conclude that the main obstacles to humane and generous migration policies are ignorance and the secrecy on which it feeds. If this report brings about a greater determination to bring the making of policy on migration into the open, it will have made a worthwhile contribution to more positive policies in the years to come.

August 1993   Professor Jack Spence
                             Director of Studies, RIIA
                         Professor George Wedell
                 Chairman of the Wyndham Place Trust

Acknowledgments

A number of people have helped greatly with the preparation of this book. Thanks must go to my colleagues at the Royal Institute of International Affairs who assisted in various ways with the project. I am particularly grateful to my department head, Dr Philip Robins, and our Director of Studies, Professor Jack Spence. Without their trusted guidance and untiring support, my job would have been a hundred times more difficult. A special thanks must also go to the members of the project steering committee, who devoted an enormous amount of time and energy to ensuring that the project ran to plan. I am also indebted to Jill Kalawoun, our programme administrator, and to Fiona Shipley of the Wyndham Place Trust, who were always there to help when the organizational side of the project got the better of me. A special thanks must also go to Margaret May and Hannah Doe of the RIIA publications department for their – as always – excellent work on the editorial and production side of the publication. I would also like to express my gratitude to the Le Poer Power Trust, the Joseph Rowntree Charitable Trust and the Beatrice Hankey Foundation, whose financial support enabled the project to go ahead. Finally, I would like to thank the academics and practitioners who took part in the Wyndham Place Trust/RIIA workshop on 'Migration into Western Europe: What Way Forward?', which was held at Chatham House in November 1992. The discussions provided considerable food for thought, and proved an important stimulus for the arguments developed here. Of course, responsibility for the information and views put forward in the book lies with the author.

August 1993   Sarah Collinson

1

Migration into Western Europe: what basis for concern?

For Western Europe, the exodus of over a million people from the East which accompanied the collapse of the Berlin Wall provided a potent symbol of the end of the Cold War. Those who 'voted with their feet' (Loescher and Scanlan, 1986) in 1989 were greeted in a climate of euphoria. They, it seemed, were responsible for the collapse of the East German state and the revolutions which swept across Eastern/Central Europe over the months that followed. They, in effect, launched Europe into what was hoped to be a new era of peace and reconciliation.

However, the very same force that heralded this transformation soon came to be seen as the new threat on our doorstep. Little more than a year later, thousands fleeing from Albania to Greece and Italy were greeted not with open arms, but with barbed wire and deportation orders. Western Europe had begun erecting new defences against the perceived threat of 'mass immigration' – thousands if not millions of people trying to use their new-found freedom to seek a more prosperous and stable life in the West. The peoples of Eastern/Central Europe had gained the right to leave their countries, but this was not to be matched with a right to enter the richer states of the West. In Albania, the barrier against entry to the West was translated directly into a new barrier against exit, as the Western embassies in Tirana were turned into fortresses and Albania's sea-ports sealed off.

According to the rhetoric of the time, the end of the Cold War paved the way to a 'New World Order'. However, the drastic

1

changes which have taken place since 1989 seem to have brought, at least for Europe, a new era of 'disorder'. The break-up of the Soviet Union and the outbreak of hostilities in Yugoslavia added to a growing sense of insecurity in Western Europe, an unease which was only heightened when the conflict in the Balkans began producing refugee flows across the borders into nearby West European states. The collapse of the Iron Curtain meant that Western Europe could no longer isolate itself from the troubles of its neighbours to the east, and nothing illustrated this state of affairs more clearly than the arrival of asylum-seekers at its doors.

The perceived immigration threat from Eastern/Central Europe and the former Soviet Union served simultaneously to draw attention to longer-standing concerns about migration from the 'South'. Since the early 1980s, the number of asylum-seekers arriving in Western Europe from the less developed world had risen substantially, those arriving in the European Community more than doubling during the latter half of the decade.[1] Coupled with this, levels of illegal and clandestine immigration, particularly into the states of Southern Europe from North and Sub-Saharan Africa, continued to increase. In Italy alone – a country which had traditionally sent migrants abroad rather than receiving them from elsewhere – the number of undocumented immigrants is estimated to exceed a quarter of a million (Rosoli, 1993:288).

Factors contributing to anxiety

Neither to the east nor to the south do the prospects for an easing of migration pressures look promising. Indeed, the pressures which could give rise to large-scale migration into Western Europe in the years to come are intensifying. In respect of Eastern/Central Europe and the former Soviet Union, there are complex problems of transition in the region, problems which are likely to result in an extended period of economic and political instability, already characterized by rising unemployment, falling living standards,

[1] In the European Community, annual asylum applications increased from 72,500 in 1985 to 170,650 in 1988, and to 558,600 in 1992. UNHCR Regional Office for the European Institutions, Brussels, January 1993.

and, in some areas, a resurgence in inter-communal tension and violence. To the south, concerns centre around rapid population growth, relative underdevelopment and/or economic stagnation, and the (linked) potential for widening and deepening political crises. All these pressures are primary factors in the generation of migration flows.

The states of Western Europe have responded to the migration 'threat' – whether real or perceived – with a strengthening of direct immigration controls, including border controls (at the so-called 'external' borders of the European Community and the European Free Trade Association, or EFTA), visa regimes, and internal surveillance mechanisms (e.g. documentation checks). However, these measures have so far failed to effect the degree of control expected of them. The long land-borders and coastlines of many states hinder effective policing of frontiers, making it difficult to prevent comparatively large numbers of migrants from entering unnoticed. Moreover, many migrants enter legally on a short-term visitor's or other visa and then remain, hoping – often with success – to avoid detection.

Control over the admission of aliens has historically been viewed as inherent in the very nature of sovereignty. Thus the spectacle of large numbers of migrants evading immigration rules provides a dramatic example of the erosion of state sovereignty in the modern world. The fact that they would have been excluded had the state been able to control their movement means that, in all probability, they are perceived as a threat and deemed 'unwanted' by much of the receiving society. Moreover, since immigrants, by definition, represent the 'outside brought within', they are liable to be regarded as a challenge to the communal integrity of the modern 'nation-state'.

Current anxiety over immigration in Western Europe may therefore be largely attributed to the general climate of insecurity following the end of the Cold War, coupled with a real decline in control over immigration flows. Additional factors have contributed to current concern, however. First, while struggling to regain control over immigration, the member states of the European

3

Community are also endeavouring to harmonize their immigration and asylum policies as part of the wider process of regional economic and political integration. As discussed in Chapter 3, the sheer complexity of this process is causing a policy overload. The difficulty of achieving swift and effective harmonization, combined with the evident failure to achieve complete control over migration flows, is drawing attention to all aspects of the issue, particularly in the media. Moreover, the fact that the harmonization process is one predicated on the maintenance of a restrictive immigration regime[2] – i.e. one in which concerns centre almost exclusively around questions of control – serves to highlight the inadequacies of present policies.

Second, it is important to note that those states which have already received large numbers of immigrants as a result of past labour recruitment policies or colonial ties (in particular, Germany, France, the United Kingdom, the Netherlands, Belgium, and Switzerland) have not yet become fully reconciled to the full social and political impacts of these past immigration flows. They are still struggling to achieve the economic and social, and to a lesser extent, political and cultural integration of settled 'immigrant' or 'minority' groups, particularly those of non-European origins, and, as discussed in Chapter 2, they are still uncertain what the desired end result of this integration process is to be. The challenges posed by the presence of large and distinct minority communities touch a raw nerve in terms of the traditional communal bases of membership in West European societies, as evidenced in the worrying upsurge in extreme anti-immigrant sentiment in a number of countries which are 'host' to such groups. The propensity for immigrant minorities to be labelled as unwanted or unwelcome is all the greater at a time of deepening economic recession and growing unemployment, when immigrant minority communities are especially prone to be seen as undeserving competitors in the market for jobs, housing and welfare benefits. As long as

[2] 'Regime' in this context signifies the institutional structure of governing arrangements set up by states to deal with the issue at the national and international levels.

4

questions concerning the status of settled immigrant minorities in Western Europe remain unresolved, governments and the public at large will continue to resist any further immigration.

Mounting concerns surrounding all aspects of immigration and refugee flows have coalesced in recent years to render migration a highly sensitive political issue. Whereas previously immigration was primarily the concern of labour and immigration ministries, it now engages the heads of states, cabinets, and ministries involved in defence, internal security and foreign policy (Weiner, 1993). It is now an issue on the agenda of the Group of Seven industrialized nations (G-7); it figures prominently in the Helsinki process; and it is discussed within the framework of the Trevi Group of European Justice and Interior Ministers and senior civil servants. The threat of large-scale migration has been used as a bargaining chip by potential sending countries in efforts to secure greater economic assistance from the West; and it is now a central concern influencing policy responses to the conflict in the former Yugoslavia.

At the same time, the issue has become more politicized at the national and regional levels as politicians attempt to respond to rising anxiety over the issue among the public at large. Recent debates on asylum in the United Kingdom and Germany indicate that even refugee policy – while never entirely divorced from political concerns – has shifted a long way into the realm of domestic politics. For example, in the United Kingdom House of Commons debate on asylum in March 1992, the then Home Secretary asserted that a new Asylum Bill was necessary so as 'not [to] give any encouragement to the rise of the extreme right in Britain'. The proposed Bill was to 'restrain the number of people who come to this country as asylum seekers. That must be the main thrust of the Government's policy and of any party's policy.'[3]

---

[3] Kenneth Baker, Hansard (House of Commons Official Report, Parliamentary Debates), vol. 205, no. 73, cols. 22 and 23–24, London, 2 March 1992.

The immigration 'threat'

Two linked assumptions appear to underlie almost all current debates on the issue of migration and refugee flows in Western Europe. First, there is the assumption that immigration poses a threat. Indeed, international migration is now one of the most widely perceived threats to Western Europe in the post-Cold War era. As such, it is an issue with a prominent place on Europe's new and changing security agenda. As observed by Weiner, 'The very form and intensity of response to unwanted migrations is itself an indication that such population flows are regarded as threats to security or stability' (Weiner, 1993). This is also reflected in the emotive nature of much of the language used in discussions of the problem. The term 'mass migration', for example, is now in common usage, although it is a phenomenon which, arguably, Western Europe has not experienced since the Second World War.

Second, it is assumed that Western Europe lacks the capacity to cope with any further immigration, whether it be in demographic, economic, social or political terms. As the European Commission observed in 1991, 'Without seeking to prejudge the question of the Member States' capacity for absorbing immigrants (which, in some cases, would seem to have reached its limits) ... the point must be to control existing immigration channels, bearing in mind that all Member States have now adopted restrictive provisions' (Commission of the European Communities, 1991:2).

Neither of these assumptions is self-evident. As regards the former, it is first necessary to identify what kinds of migration are being talked of before attempting to reach any clear conclusions as to whether immigration might, or might not, pose a threat to the receiving countries. For example, immigration may take place suddenly or gradually, it may be uncontrolled or managed, legal or illegal, temporary or permanent, it may involve skilled or unskilled workers, Europeans or non-Europeans.[4] In Britain, for instance, considerable concern may be expressed about illegal Bangladeshi immigrants working in the 'sweat-shops' of the East

[4] For a rough typology of different kinds of migration, see Collinson, 1993:2–3.

6

End of London, but Australians working illegally in the wine-bars and pubs of West London attract hardly any attention at all (Owers, 1993). Each type of immigration is likely to have quite specific impacts on the receiving country which do not apply to immigration flows in general.

Until these impacts – whether actual or potential – have been clearly identified, it is difficult to assert that a country has reached its immigration capacity. To gauge a country's absorptive capacity, it is first necessary to consider what kinds of immigration might create tensions, to examine what these tensions are likely to be, and to question what factors might influence the nature and extent of these strains. Furthermore, it may not be entirely helpful to limit consideration to the national or supra-national level. The European Community or any one member state may well have the capacity to cope with much larger immigration flows than are being experienced at present. That may not be the case, however, for particular regions or localities, or for particular sectors of the labour and housing markets. As the impact of immigration is rarely uniform across all sectors of society, different concerns may arise from different sectors. Thus, the worries expressed by members of the political elite (e.g. over the impact of large Islamic minority communities) may not be the same as fears expressed by those more directly affected by immigration (e.g. over the pressure on the availability of housing).

Similarly, in order to judge whether immigration poses a threat for Western Europe, it is necessary to question just what kinds of threats are envisaged. Arguments for restricting immigration, at least those voiced by policy-makers, generally centre on one or more of four basic concerns: first, the possible negative effect on the economy; second, the possible negative impact on the integration of immigrant minority groups; third, the potential internal security threats; and fourth, the apparent threat to the existing social, cultural and political order, i.e. the perceived challenge to values regarded as the basis of identity or membership of the receiving society in question. Although no across-the-board conclusions can be reached as to the potential problems posed by immigration, a

7

few broad observations deserve mention inasmuch as they challenge some of the assumptions upon which these perceived threats are premised.

Economic concerns

The economic arguments against further immigration are far from clear-cut. As discussed in Chapter 3, labour market trends in Western Europe suggest the likelihood of a continuing demand for workers in the years to come which will not be readily satisfied by the indigenous labour force, despite economic recession and high levels of unemployment. Moreover, existing research suggests that immigrants, whether entering legally or illegally, may have, at worst, a neutral impact on the receiving state's economy, irrespective of demographic or structural demands.[5] Possible positive economic effects may be particularly marked in regions or localities where immigrants become concentrated, owing to their direct contribution to local production and consumption. This may hold even in conditions of relatively high unemployment, in part because immigrants (particularly illegal immigrants) often accept the kinds of jobs which are shunned by members of the indigenous community (including the unemployed). As Julian Simon has observed in the context of immigration in the United States:

> Several recent studies have tackled the matter of 'displacement' empirically using a variety of approaches. No study has found across-the-board unemployment caused by immigrants, either in the US as a whole or in particular areas of relatively high immigration. In addition, effects on particular groups are surprisingly small or non-existent, even groups such as blacks and women in California who are seemingly at special risk from Mexican immigrants. In short, immigrants not only take jobs, they make jobs. They create new

[5] See the findings of recent research carried out in Germany, as presented in papers prepared for the seminar on the Economic and Social Impact of Migration organized by the Institute for Public Policy Research and Friedrich Ebert Foundation, London, March 1993.

jobs indirectly with their spending. They also create new jobs directly with the businesses which they are more likely than natives to start (Simon, 1993:115–16).

A number of reservations ought to be noted in this context, however. First, much depends on the specific economic conditions prevailing in the sector, locality or country into which immigration takes place at any time, and on the nature of the immigration flows themselves, and for this reason generalization is extremely problematic.

Second, the local economic benefits of immigration may well be countered by elements of 'congestion', such as housing shortages in receiving areas. The larger and more sudden the immigration flow, the more significant these factors are likely to be, although in the longer term one might expect the housing market and other slow-responding elements of the economy to 'catch up' with the new demand.

Third, at the national level, it is possible that certain kinds of immigration will have a distorting effect on the economy. Certainly during the early 1970s labour immigration was blamed for a failure to develop more modern, capital-intensive forms of production in the major receiving states; and today, one can identify a clear link between the strength of the 'informal economy' in Southern Europe and levels of illegal immigration into the region. This, however, is something of a 'chicken-or-egg' question. To the extent that immigration is generated by demand in the receiving country, it becomes an issue of labour market as well as immigration policies (see Chapter 3).

The fourth reservation concerns the strains that immigrant communities may exert on state welfare provision. Such an argument can only be put very tentatively, however, as the demands that immigrants make on public spending will vary considerably from group to group and country to country, and are likely to change considerably over time. Moreover, while immigrant minorities may make particularly heavy demands on one part of the system (e.g. education and health), their pressure on other areas may be well below that of the 'indigenous' population (e.g. care for the elderly). Furthermore, what immigrants contribute as taxpayers may frequently outweigh the public resources they 'consume' as beneficiaries of the system.

Fifth, a recognition of the potential economic benefits of immigration at the local level needs to be balanced against social and political concerns when immigrants enter positions in marginal and unregulated sectors of the labour market where they are likely to suffer exploitation and/or poor working conditions. Again, this is a question which concerns labour-market policies.

On balance, it is not at all obvious that higher levels of immigration into Western Europe would have overwhelmingly negative effects on receiving states' economies. Indeed, there is considerable evidence to suggest that the overall economic impact might be positive.[6] To support this view, it is worth noting that 'economic' migration in the narrow sense is, in essence, an expression of market forces. Classical liberal economic theory supports free movement, on the basis that markets function most effectively when there is 'no exercise of constraint over any individual by another individual or "society" ... that is, [when there is] ... "perfect mobility"' (Knight, 1921:77). Recognition of the economic value of free movement was expressed in the EEC Treaty of Rome which, according to Article 48, secured the free movement of workers within the European Community, a provision subsequently expanded to the free movement of persons[7] by Article 8a of the Single European Act.

[6] Note that research carried out in Germany over recent years suggests that immigration since 1989 has had a positive effect on the German economy, although it should be stressed that the findings cannot be extrapolated into the future. See the papers presented at the Institute for Public Policy Research/Friedrich Ebert Foundation seminar on the Economic and Social Impact of Migration, March 1993.
[7] To be interpreted as the free movement of *citizens*, for third-country nationals are excluded from the rights of free movement and establishment accorded to EC nationals.

Social and political concerns
However, just as migration is shaped by much more than economic forces, so migration policy reflects more than pure economic interest. As observed by Böhning, 'In the sphere of international economic migration, central governments tend to pay more attention to noneconomic factors than in the spheres of trade or monetary flows, because the moves of people affect the innermost feelings of nations' (Böhning, 1981:31). Thus, whether or not future immigration might benefit the economies of Western Europe, attention must be given to some of the other concerns underlying the current resistance to, and indeed fear of, immigration.

A further concern of policy-makers, noted above, is that a resumption of large-scale immigration might threaten the still fragile processes of immigrant integration in Western Europe. This is an argument which has been voiced continually by the governments of every receiving state since the halt on labour immigration in the 1970s, and which, in today's climate, is stressed more forcefully than ever. As stated by the European Commission in 1991, 'better control of migration flows' is 'the prerequisite for any harmonious integration' (Commission of the European Communities, 1991:9). At first sight, this argument would appear self-evident, based on the assumption that society's capacity to absorb large and distinct minorities is limited by an inherent resistance to social, political and cultural change. The current rise in extreme anti-immigrant opinion in Germany and elsewhere in Western Europe, for example, is commonly blamed solely and explicitly on high levels of immigration. When speaking of the dramatic rise in the vote for the extreme right Republikaner party in Germany in April 1992, the then UK Home Secretary stated that it was due to one issue, that being 'the flood of migrants and would-be asylum seekers whose continuing numbers have aroused public concern'.[8]

However, the nexus between integration and immigration control may not be quite as straightforward as this assumption would lead one to believe. If one considers that a country's

[8] Kenneth Baker, as quoted by Robert Maclennan, MP. See Hansard, vol. 209, no. 23, col. 174 (8 June 1992).

absorptive capacity is influenced by prevailing attitudes about what constitutes 'membership' of a society, or what forms the foundations of national cohesion, one is led to question how immigration policy itself may influence these attitudes, and thus how immigration policy may in turn influence levels of toleration in society. Put simply, an excessively restrictive immigration policy regime implies a sharp dividing line between 'insiders' and 'outsiders' in society which, in the presence of large immigrant minority communities, does not really exist. Strict immigration controls could be seen implicitly to label immigrants in general – and, to the extent that controls impact on some groups more than others, certain immigrant minorities in particular – as unwelcome and as 'outsiders', a label which may be registered not only by the immigrants themselves, but also by members of the wider public. It is quite possible that this will have a substantive effect on both immigrants' and the wider public's perceptions of who does and does not 'belong'. Such perceptions could inhibit or undermine the process of integration which is regarded as so important for future political and social cohesion and stability. The argument may have more to do with how the objectives of immigration control are conveyed to the public by governments and other authorities than it does with the actual operation of immigration controls,[9] but it remains valid nonetheless.

Relevant to this argument are two (overlapping) concerns noted earlier, namely, the potential direct security threats posed by immigration, and the perceived challenge that immigration brings to the existing social, cultural and political order. Of all the arguments invoked as a basis for restricting immigration, the latter may be seen as the most spurious, as it is linked so closely with a nationalist form of ideology which appears less and less appropriate in the context of modern-day Europe. Nonetheless, it cannot be discounted, as it is possibly one of the most pervasive elements shaping current immigration policy. The importance of registering

[9] Note, for example, that settled immigrants may themselves support strict controls on certain categories of immigration, especially on worker immigration.

this concern is highlighted by Zolberg, who notes that international migration is generally seen to constitute 'a deviance from the prevailing norm of social organization at the world level', and that this norm is reflected

> not only in the popular conception of a world consisting of reified countries considered as nearly natural entities, but also in the conceptual apparatus common to all the social sciences, predicated on a model of society as a territorially-based, self-reproducing cultural and social system, whose human population is assumed ... to renew itself endogenously over an indefinite period ... [T]he perennial intrusion of racial and ethnic considerations in the determination of immigration policies is not merely the consequence of prejudice ... but the effect of systemic mechanisms whereby societies seek to preserve their boundaries in a world populated by others, some of whom are deemed particularly threatening in the light of prevailing cultural orientations (Zolberg, 1981:6&11).

Clues to the significance of these concerns can be found in the overarching effort to integrate existing immigrant groups, while immigrants' access to citizenship and political rights continues to be restricted (Hammar, 1990; Layton-Henry, 1990; Baubock, 1992). These concerns are also indicated by policy statements which frequently reveal something of a regret that past large-scale immigration took place, and in the thrust of current 'initiatives' in immigration policy, which exhibit more of a concern to maintain the *status quo* than they do a willingness to engage in a critical examination and re-evaluation of the traditional concepts which have guided policy up until now. The fact that such a basis for immigration policy is problematic is reflected in the ideological difficulties which beset the concept of a 'Fortress Europe' (i.e. its uneasy relationship with liberal thinking). West European society as a whole has already undergone changes over recent decades which make it impossible to continue to view it as a composite of neatly bounded cultural, social, ethnic and political units.

In this context, it is worth noting that, at a time when states' sovereignty is being eroded by a wide range of transnational economic and political forces, governments are likely to be on the defensive against any development which appears further to undermine their countries' sovereignty. They can be expected to be particularly sensitive about 'unwanted' immigration, not only because it challenges one of the fundamental hallmarks of state sovereignty (control of state borders and the movement of aliens across those borders), but also because it may be seen to challenge the basis of 'national' social and political cohesion upon which the integrity of the nation-state ostensibly depends. The latter challenge may be regarded as more direct and immediate than would be suggested by the somewhat diffuse concern over immigrants' potential impact on the 'national identity', and in this respect, the interest in maintaining social and political cohesion overlaps with the concern to maintain internal security.

Security concerns
There are a number of ways in which immigration may be seen to threaten a country's security. The most obvious derives from the issue of 'tolerance'. A society's capacity to cope with an immigration flow is determined both by the particular social, economic and political conditions prevailing in the receiving country or receiving region affected, and by the specific qualitative and quantitative characteristics of that migration flow. However difficult this capacity may be to measure, and however much it may vary from one situation to another, it is a fact of life that a society's tolerance of immigration has, at some point, an upper threshold beyond which strains will begin to appear, whether they be economic, social or political in nature.

The fact that the historical development of West European society took place mainly in the absence of large racially, ethnically, culturally and religiously distinct immigrant communities, and the fact that population density is relatively high, suggest that tolerance levels, at least within certain sectors of society, may be lower than in the traditional immigration countries, such as Canada, the

14

United States and Australia. The recent increase in extreme anti-immigrant opinion in Western Europe – less prevalent in the traditional immigration countries – would seem to support this view. Although anti-immigrant attitudes may not be solely or directly attributable to continuing immigration, governments will be reluctant to allow immigration to continue if they consider this likely to aggravate such attitudes. These pose a security threat, not only through their direct link with violence, but also through their potential for opening up new or latent cleavages in society.

However, the 'threat to security' is a somewhat nebulous and shifting construct which becomes particularly difficult to pinpoint when premised upon actual or potential forces in society which are neither easy to identify or predict, nor easy to explain. It may, for example, seem obvious that rising xenophobia in Germany is linked directly to the number of asylum-seekers currently entering the country. Yet it is possible that the cause of this insecurity – which at present is expressed through violence against foreigners – has less to do with immigration, and far more to do with the pressures and strains of unification and the processes of economic, political and social transformation in eastern Germany.

There are, however, two respects in which the immigration–security link may be seen as more concrete, both of which derive from the observation that immigrants represent 'the outside brought within'. First, although immigrants generally forge new attachments to the receiving country and society, they very rarely detach themselves entirely from their country of origin, whether economically, politically or culturally. Indeed, a number of studies carried out over recent years indicate that immigrant minority populations often remain very sensitive to developments in the country of origin.[10] From this observation derives the possibility that immigrant groups may render the receiving state more vulnerable to developments in the sending countries or elsewhere which would otherwise remain almost entirely external. The Salman Rushdie affair provides one example, as do signs of the potential

[10] See, for example, Rex et al., 1987.

radicalization of North African minorities in France and elsewhere in Western Europe as a result of a rise in religious fervour in the Maghreb.

Second, the presence of certain immigrant groups may strain relations between the receiving country and the country of origin: for example, if immigrants are opposed to the regime of their host country (e.g. Turkish Kurds in Germany), or if the country of origin is unhappy about the treatment of its nationals in the host state (e.g. Turkey's current concerns about the protection of Turkish nationals in Germany). Moreover, the presence of immigrant minorities may exert an additional strain on the foreign policy decisions of the 'host' state (note, for example, the unrest manifest among a number of Muslim immigrant groups during the Gulf war).

The security concern may be the most persuasive of all arguments upon which resistance to 'unwanted' migration is based. However, the security implications of any migration flow are likely to be context-specific, thus unpredictable, and, to a great extent, symptomatic of broader internal or external developments of which migration is just one part.[11] Moreover, the kinds of internal security concerns mentioned above may divert attention from potentially more worrying security questions connected with migration flows and migration pressures. Refugee or 'involuntary' flows provide a case in point, which is all the more salient because an examination of migration pressures building up in areas surrounding Western Europe reveals that these kinds of flows may well become dominant in the years and decades to come. Sudden, involuntary migration movements, particularly large-scale flows, are almost certainly the most disruptive and traumatic of all types of migration, and it is therefore natural to argue that they should be prevented wherever possible. However, by instituting policies which are predicated simply on an interest to protect the internal security of the receiving country – i.e. by introducing restrictive

[11] Note, for example, political tensions between Albania and Greece at the time of writing, which were exacerbated by the Greek government's expulsion of over 20,000 Albanians in July 1993. See *The Independent*, 30 June 1993; *International Herald Tribune*, 2 July 1993; *The Guardian*, 3 July 1993.

policies which prevent refugees from gaining entry – the states of Western Europe run the risk of creating new external security threats. For example, external political or economic instability may result if necessary refugee flows are prevented,[12] or if substantial refugee flows are deflected to, or allowed to become concentrated in, poorer and less stable countries whose capacity to cope is more limited.[13]

Looking ahead

Today's receiving states are more likely than not to view most immigration – particularly uncontrolled immigration – as undesirable, whether due to economic, social, political or security concerns. However, the fact that what are already very restrictive immigration policies are failing to prevent much unwelcome immigration leads one to wonder whether different measures might not be called for. Current restrictionist thinking may be simply too rigid and too narrow for a number of potentially important policy questions even to be considered. International migration is an extremely complex phenomenon, and correspondingly complex equations need to be worked out if the pros and cons of immigration in all its various guises, and the balance of advantages of different forms of control or management, are to be identified.

[12] Necessary for the survival of the individuals concerned.
[13] Note also, in the context of refugees from conflict, the potential for refugee populations to remain concentrated in areas affected by the conflict, thereby potentially exacerbating political tensions in the region. See Loescher, 1992b.

17

2

Integration, ethnicity and multiculturalism in Western Europe

Migration is not a new phenomenon for Western Europe. Indeed, the history of Europe over the centuries has been one of more or less continuous migration. As Jorgen Nielsen observes, European culture would not be what it is had it not been for the constant 'intellectual, artistic, spiritual and technological cross-fertilisation' mediated by the movement of people (Nielsen, 1992:151). However, the postwar era seems to have marked a watershed in Europe's migration history. The break appears to have been so significant as to wipe most previous migration from the collective memory. What set the new migration apart from earlier flows was that it involved not only European populations, but also large numbers of migrants from more distant countries and more distant cultures. Europe was soon host to significant immigrant populations of a kind which, in terms of the social and political challenges they posed, seemed to have no precedent.

This new migration stream did not come about spontaneously. It was encouraged, or at least sanctioned, by the receiving states of northwestern Europe, hungry as they were for cheap labour. Economic interest overshadowed almost all other considerations, and thus, somewhat surprisingly, it was not until after nearly a decade of large-scale immigration that politicians in general began to show an open concern with the social and political implications of this influx. With the recessions of the late 1960s and early 1970s, it became clear that most of the new immigrant populations were 'here for good' (Castles et al., 1984). They could not be treated as a disposable economic resource, but were people who had forged new links with the receiving country and who could not be removed *en masse* except by force. No receiving state was prepared to embark on a programme of enforced repatriation, and incentive-based return programmes, such as those pursued by France after 1977 and Germany after 1982, had very little impact (Collinson, 1993:60–61). Thus attention turned towards the integration of immigrant workers and their families, the latter, in particular, continuing to represent an important immigration stream.

Immigrant integration
The need to integrate Europe's 'immigrant communities' has been stated and restated by policy-makers ever since the halt on worker immigration which followed the 1973 oil crisis. However, the term 'immigrant communities' raises important questions of definition. It is becoming increasingly misleading to use the label 'immigrants', as these communities now include a growing contingent of second- and third-generation members who have been born and brought up in the country of residence. Moreover, large numbers of postwar migrants in Europe tend to escape notice because of their European origins (e.g. Irish residents in Britain). Different terms have come to be employed in different countries to denote those groups for which integration is seen as a problem: in Britain it is usual to talk of 'ethnic minorities', in Germany it is 'foreigners' or 'aliens', and in France it is common to refer to 'immigrants' or 'populations of foreign origin'. The various terms reveal much about differing perceptions of these groups' place in society (Collinson, 1993).

However, there is a common element linking the discourse in every country: a concern with communities which are both economically disadvantaged and which display a distinct 'ethnicity' based on a culture, race, religion, language and/or national identity with roots elsewhere. It is not the immigrant status of these groups which seems to matter so much as their cultural, racial or religious 'difference' from the receiving society, reinforced by social and economic marginalization. Thus it is on communities of immigrant origin which are at once visible and disadvantaged that integration policies have focused. As expressed recently in a report for the European Commission on immigration policies and the social integration of migrants, 'Integration is inescapable as a policy if we are setting out to defuse the tensions inherent in the immigration of generally poor, inadequately equipped and ethnically different people' (Commission of the European Communities, 1990:14).

Since the early to mid-1980s, there has been a growing recognition, at least in principle, that efforts are needed to strengthen and improve immigrant minorities' social and economic rights and opportunities. This is reflected in the European Commission's report on integration, which stresses the need for greater security of stay for immigrants and their offspring, and the need for action in the areas of employment and business, education and housing. It is argued that integration, when understood as a process which prevents or counteracts the social marginalization of immigrants, 'leaves aside the somewhat heated but sterile debate on assimilation versus multiculturalism' as social integration is necessary irrespective of whether assimilationist[1] or multicultural[2] policies are pursued (Commission of the European Communities, 1990).

Yet if integration is simply a question of improving immigrant minorities' social and economic status, one is led to question what it is that sets immigrants apart from other disadvantaged groups in society. To a large extent, immigrant disadvantage is synonymous with class disadvantage: most immigrant workers originally entered positions in the labour market which placed them firmly within the working class, and thus their present socio-economic position may be largely explained in terms of their class position.[3]

[1] Understood as policies designed to minimize all forms of cultural and/or religious difference.
[2] Understood in its simplest form as a policy which supports or encourages multiple forms of (group-based) cultural expression in society.
[3] For a discussion of how initial entry into the labour market affects immigrants' position in society, see Piore, 1979. For a discussion of immigrants' class status in Britain, see Miles and Phizacklea, 1977; and in the European context, Castles and Kosack, 1973.

Why, therefore, should integration policies differ from wider policies designed to counter all forms of class-based disadvantage? It is interesting to note that in the Netherlands and the United Kingdom, a number of 'urban regeneration' and other policies designed either directly or indirectly to improve the social and economic status of immigrant minorities have actually exploited this linkage so as to prevent the resentment that might arise within other sectors of the population if policies were seen to favour minorities. Indeed, as Van Praag notes, in the Netherlands it is unclear whether foreign origin or deprivation is the primary criterion in selecting the groups to which 'minority policy' applies (Van Praag, 1986:40; Netherlands Scientific Council for Government Policy, 1990:40).

Yet, while class status is undoubtedly a central factor explaining the position of immigrant minorities in Western Europe, it is not the only one to be considered, and it should also be noted that immigrant and ethnic minorities' socio-economic status varies considerably. Even those policies aimed at improving immigrants' social and economic mobility have run up against a number of problems behind which lie important questions relating to immigrants' 'ethnicity'. This becomes clear once one ventures into the realms of culture, political rights and the issue of citizenship.

Integration and 'ethnicity'

The importance of the ethnicity issue in shaping integration policy has been marked in Western Europe since the early 1970s (Collinson, 1993). European receiving states have demonstrated varying ways of working around the issue, ranging from direct efforts to minimize cultural difference ('assimilation' policies, as in France during the 1970s and early 1980s), to avoidance[4] (Germany, and France during the 1950s and 1960s), toleration[5] (United Kingdom), through

[4] Meaning that no national policy was developed which dealt either directly or indirectly with the cultural question.
[5] Meaning that considerable room was allowed for cultural difference, but that no consistent and explicit policy was developed to support or encourage cultural difference at the national level.

to direct encouragement[6] ('multicultural' policies, as in the Netherlands and Sweden). The various models which emerged grew largely out of *ad hoc* and reactive responses which differed according to the varying experiences of immigration itself and the particular political culture and structures in place in each receiving state. It is too early to tell where the 'new' immigration countries of Southern Europe[7] will slot in along this axis or, indeed, where the countries listed are likely to settle in the years to come. Certainly, in terms of official policy, the drift would seem to be towards the centre (toleration). However, this may not be the case if anti-immigrant opinion increases its influence in mainstream politics, as has recently been noticeable in France, Belgium and Austria.

In France, an initial assumption that social, economic and cultural integration would take place automatically without the help of state institutions was later replaced by an active (and highly centralized) policy to encourage immigrants to 'assimilate' to French cultural norms. This policy was based on the insistence on a direct and unified identification with the French state which precluded the recognition of minorities. However, during the late 1980s and early 1990s, the government was more open to recognizing the reality of cultural heterogeneity, and moved towards a more liberal approach, particularly in education, in an attempt to ease growing inter-ethnic tensions in French society.

For the Germans, the notion that theirs is 'not an immigration country', combined with the myth of migrant ('guest-') worker rotation and return, meant that the integration question was avoided for longer. Throughout the 1960s and 1970s, immigrants were effectively segregated from mainstream society. In practice, this resulted in a largely *laissez-faire* attitude to immigrants' cultural and religious expression. In some *Länder*, this verged on an active encouragement of immigrant identity maintenance, as this,

[6] That is, policies which lent explicit support to cultural difference.
[7] Meaning the states of Southern Europe, particularly Italy and Spain, and to a lesser extent Greece and Portugal. These countries have traditionally sent migrants abroad, and it is only over the past decade or so that they have begun to experience significant levels of immigration. See Collinson, 1993.

it was believed, would ease migrants' eventual return to their country of origin. More recent policy initiatives, at least those at the federal level, reveal a growing preoccupation with so-called second- and third-generation 'foreigners', but little in the way of an overall ideological framework to guide policy beyond a concern to improve their social and economic status.[8]

In Britain, the majority of postwar immigrants entered the country as British subjects with full citizenship rights.[9] There was therefore no question of Britain sanctioning a system of institutionalized segregation such as that which emerged in Germany. In contrast to France, it was race rather than culture which emerged as the most salient problem, and this led to a series of Race Relations Acts which put in place an enforceable framework of legislation to protect ethnic minorities from direct and indirect discrimination in all areas of public life. The official government line has tended to lay stress on 'equal opportunities', according to which policy is directed towards shaping society so that everyone 'can participate freely and fully in the economic, social and public life of the nation while having the freedom to maintain their own religious and cultural identity' (Home Office, 1990).

British policy has sometimes been described as multicultural because of the opportunities allowed for minority cultural autonomy, and because a number of local authorities have adopted a more multicultural line than has central government, particularly in the field of education. However, Britain has never adopted an explicitly multicultural policy, tending to favour a more 'hands-off' approach to cultural matters. Only in the Netherlands and, to a lesser extent, Sweden has central government attempted to translate an explicit endorsement of multicultural values into a

[8] See, for example, Federal Minister of the Interior, 1991.
[9] Under the 1948 Nationality Act, all colonial and Commonwealth citizens were British subjects, and, as such, were free to hold a UK passport, to enter Britain to find work, to settle and to bring families without being subject to immigration controls. Once in the UK, all UK passport holders had the same rights and duties, including the right to vote in local and national elections. See Collinson, 1993:49.

coherent policy framework. In the Netherlands, such an approach seemed to fit in well with the country's pluralist traditions, discussion even turning at times to the possibility of encouraging the formation of a Muslim 'pillar' to match those of the Christian Churches and established secular or humanist bodies. The government has thus accepted some responsibility for helping minorities preserve, develop and express their cultural identity, based on the notion that a strong group identity would help them overcome their social and economic disadvantage (Netherlands Scientific Council for Government Policy, 1990).

Recent developments point to some of the more fundamental problems which beset 'immigrant' or 'minority' policies in Western Europe. In the Netherlands, there has been a retreat from the multicultural stance of the past in favour of anti-deprivation and anti-discrimination policies, as the earlier stance not only seemed to be failing in terms of improving the socio-economic position of immigrant minorities, but also became more difficult to support as anti-immigrant feeling began to rise during the early 1980s (Netherlands Scientific Council for Government Policy, 1990). In Britain, equivocal attitudes towards the status of immigrant culture, and particularly non-Christian religions, were made explicit in 1988 with the passing of the Education Reform Act which requires a 'mainly or broadly Christian content in religious education and school worship'. According to Jorgen Nielsen, the exceptions made for schools in which ethnic minority pupils predominate may only have served to strengthen feelings of marginality among Muslims and other non-Christians (Nielsen, 1992:160). The 'Rushdie affair' of 1989/90 increased this tension, raising as it did fundamental questions about the role of Islam (and religion in general) in public life, and revealing a comprehension gap between sections of the Muslim community and the rest of society.

Equally difficult questions were brought to the fore by the 'headscarves affair' in France. This issue took on great symbolic importance there, not least because it coincided with the Republic's bicentenary celebrations in 1989. The girls' insistence on covering their heads at school for religious reasons was seen as a direct challenge to the republican and lay identity of the French state (Nielsen, 1992:163). Two years after the government passed a law prohibiting the display of distinctive religious, political or ideological symbols in school, the *Conseil d'Etat* ruled that freedom of expression should not be jeopardized by the secular principles of education and that the girls should therefore be able to wear their headscarves (Gaeremynck, 1993).[10]

The variations and shifts in approaches to the cultural dimension of immigrant status in themselves indicate the difficulties that European receiving states have had in coming to terms with the presence of culturally, ethnically or religiously distinct immigrant minority communities. Today's problems may be seen to stem less from continuing immigration (with the exception of the 'new' immigration countries of Southern Europe) than from a failure throughout the past four decades to reach a clear vision of what immigration means for the future of West European societies, particularly for the basis of communal identity, whether that be national identity or the now increasingly popular concept of a 'European identity'. A number of basic questions still need to be addressed, including those formulated by Peter Schuck in the context of the United States: 'Who are we? What do we wish to become? Which individuals can help us reach that goal? Which individuals constitute the "we" who shall decide these questions?' (Schuck, 1985:286; Schmitter Heisler, 1992:641).

'Multiculturalism' as a model
As European governments have begun to acknowledge the reality of cultural, ethnic and religious diversity, it has become increasingly common to refer to these societies as multicultural. A recent report on the Council of Europe's Community Relations project, for example, states that 'The presence of immigrant communities and their growth have undoubtedly reinforced the multicultural character of European society.' The report goes on to observe that 'Most immigration countries in Western Europe have discovered

---

[10] See also *Libération*, 3 November 1992.

the strength of ethnicity' and that 'It has been acknowledged that immigration has indeed led to the development of multi-ethnic societies' (Council of Europe, 1991).

The concept of multiculturalism remains very vague, however, at least in the European context. As Isajiw has argued, 'one must distinguish between multiculturalism as an ideology, a social policy, and as a feature of the structure of society' (Isajiw, 1975:1; Schmitter Heisler, 1992:633). As is already clear, multiculturalism as a coherent social policy has a long way to go in Western Europe. As a feature of social structure, Western Europe is certainly multicultural in the sense that a number of different cultures are present in society. However, if used in this sense, the term is devoid of any meaning other than an indication of cultural diversity. It says nothing about how this diversity is structured in society. Indeed, even as an ideology, the concept requires clarification, for, as John Rex has argued, a look at the various forms of plural 'multi-cultural' and 'multi-racial' societies in the world reveals that 'such societies are far from providing us with an ideal and it must therefore be in some very special sense that we speak of such an ideal in contemporary conditions' (Rex, 1985:3).

Jorgen Nielsen writes of the 'liberal myth of multicultural Europe', and argues that those who lay too much stress on the multicultural nature of European society fail to take on board the significance of the nation as a central ideological and political construct in Western Europe. Indeed, he argues that to talk of Europe's 'new' multicultural identity implicitly legitimates the ideal of the culturally bounded nation by affirming the 'common European myth of a pre-existent monocultural society'. The 'monocultural myth of the national culture' in his eyes 'predisposes it against a multicultural ideal', and thus, he argues, the social reality of multicultural Europe is one in which immigrant culture becomes a sub-culture beneath the dominant national culture; in which these sub-cultures are tolerated only as long as they do not impinge on the life of the majority; and in which any adaptation necessary must be effected by the minorities rather than the majority as it is the bearers of European native culture who also hold the instruments of political, economic and social control (Nielsen, 1992:150–53).

Yet, according to Ernest Gellner, advanced industrial societies such as those of Western Europe depend on a shared unitary culture at national or state level. The essential characteristics of industrial society – including universal literacy, mobility and individualism, political centralization, and a costly state-supervised educational infrastructure – 'impel it into a situation in which political and cultural boundaries are on the whole congruent' (Gellner, 1983:110).

What is essential about this shared culture is that it is a 'high' culture, i.e. that it is based on 'standardized, literacy- and education-based systems of communication' (Gellner, 1983:54), for its primary importance is in the 'public' domain of politics and economics. In other respects, it may vary considerably. In the modern world, it is generally incorporated into forms of 'national' culture or identification. Yet, as Anthony Smith argues, the concept of 'national identity' itself takes many forms. This is illustrated by what have been termed the 'Western' and 'Eastern' models of national identity: the 'Western' model based on 'historic territory, legal-political community, legal-political equality of members, and common civic culture and ideology'; and the 'Eastern' model based on 'genealogy and presumed descent ties, popular mobilization, vernacular languages, customs and traditions' (Smith, 1991:11&12). These may be taken as 'ideal types', for in the real world, every national identity incorporates both civic ('Western') and ethnic ('Eastern') elements in varying forms and to varying extents (Smith, 1991:13).

Gellner's conception of the unified national culture does not preclude cultural difference within a state, but precludes cultural difference which is politically and/or economically significant in the public domain. Drawing on the twin concepts of the unified 'high' national culture and the 'Western' model of national identity, John Rex puts forward a model for multiculturalism which does not conflict with the concept of political and cultural unity at the national level (Rex, 1985). The model is based on the principle of equality of rights, and is therefore distinguished very clearly from what he terms a 'plural' model, in which ethnic or cultural cleavages coincide with a differentiated structure of social, economic, civil and political rights. The public domain, including the world of law, politics, economics and education,[11] is governed by a single high 'civic culture' based upon the notion of the political and legal equality of individuals. Cultural diversity or 'folk culture' is restricted to, but allowed to flourish in, the private domain, this being responsible for 'moral education, primary socialization and the inculcation of religious belief'.

A similar model is also advocated in the Council of Europe report on community relations, where it is stated that:

> It has been acknowledged that immigration has ... led to the development of multi-ethnic societies and that such societies should offer possibilities for peaceful coexistence to all communities, thus enabling people to arrange their private lives in line with their own traditions, within the limits set by the existing legal order (which in itself is not unchangeable). Such relatively pluralist views are based on the idea that, in the private sphere at least, cultures can be compatible and that different cultures and ethnic communities can live together peacefully in one and the same society (Council of Europe, 1991:22).

Yet, whereas this report stresses the potential for 'peaceful coexistence' in such a structure, Rex takes note of the potential for conflict. He argues that 'civic culture includes the notion of conflict. The social order which we have is the resultant of conflict ... minority communities at any one time may conflict with and challenge the existing order as have communities based upon social class in the past' (Rex, 1985:15–16).

'Multicultural society' in Western Europe

Collective identities have never been fixed, but are constantly reinvented and reconstructed. The extent to which a more pluralist

[11] Education restricted to a public role, i.e. the transmission of skills and public values.

conception of the nation has developed in Western Europe during the second half of this century (albeit unevenly) would seem to bode well for the development of multicultural society as envisaged by Rex. It would seem to be linked with a weakening of exclusivist nationalist sentiment in the public sphere and its gradual replacement by a more inclusive and rational civic culture governing relations between individuals and sub-groups in society.

However, Western Europe clearly has a long way to go before it can be said that its societies fit such a multicultural model. Perhaps most importantly, one is led to question the extent to which the public domain is structured purely on the basis of a civic culture. To what extent are national communities held together in the public sphere by rational ties based on organized political and economic association and 'the praxis of citizens who actively exercise their civil rights' (Habermas, 1991), and to what extent by affective 'bonds of solidarity among members ... united by shared memories, myths and traditions' (Smith, 1991:15) and ethnic and wider cultural and/or religious ties? The balance between these cohesive forces differs from country to country, but in no country in Western Europe has affective culture entirely given way to civic values in the public domain.

For example, in Germany there still exists a very strong attachment to the concept of the German *Volk*. Thus, German ethnicity tends to play a dominant role in both the private and the public spheres, as reflected in Germany's very restrictive citizenship policies.[12] In Britain, there is no constitutional separation between Church and state. Therefore, despite the fact that British society today may be described as predominantly secular or post-Christian, at the institutional level the Christian religion is still accorded

---

[12] Note that German citizenship has traditionally been based on the principle of *jus sanguinis*, i.e. ethnic ties. For this reason, 'ethnic Germans' from Eastern and Central Europe have had little difficulty in acquiring German citizenship. However, as regards other groups, not only first-generation immigrants, but also the majority of their offspring born in Germany, remain unnaturalized owing to the juridical and administrative barriers to naturalization. Moves are now under way to amend Germany's citizenship laws to make naturalization easier. See, for example, *Migration News Sheet*, July 1993; and *Frankfurter Allgemeine Zeitung*, 1 July 1993.

an important role in the public sphere and it is held on to as an important symbol of (English) national identity. In France, one might expect to find the clearest representation of a nation united on the basis of civic culture as a result of the post-Revolutionary emphasis on a unitary 'political culture' to replace the various regional or ethnic cultures. However, this political culture was never devoid of 'ethnic' content, and foreign immigrants have been expected to assimilate culturally (at least in the past) to much more than basic civic values.

A more concrete deviation from the multicultural model is evident in the extent to which immigrant minorities *as groups* are differentially incorporated socially, economically and politically in both *de facto* and *de jure* terms in Western Europe. In this respect, West European society might be seen to come closer to representing Rex's 'plural' model, in which ethnic or cultural cleavages coincide with a differentiated structure of social, economic, civil and political rights and opportunities.

The multicultural model envisaged by Rex depends on no individual having 'more or less rights than any other or a greater or lesser capacity to operate in this world of conflict because of his or her ethnic category'. Yet access to, and exercise of, rights has always depended on the individual's citizenship status, defined not only in formal but also in substantive terms. This should pose no problems when it is clear who are and who are not 'members' or citizens. However, the very same process which has made multiculturalism a salient issue in Western Europe has also brought about an erosion of the distinction between members and non-members, and between citizens and 'foreigners'. As observed by Layton-Henry:

> The settlement of foreign migrant workers in Western Europe has caused a reassessment of the concept of membership of a modern state. In the pre-war period, almost all members of European states were citizens with full legal, civil and political rights, but now many members of Western democracies are not citizens. They are certainly members of

these states participating in the labour and housing markets, paying taxes, bringing up families and sending their children to school ... In some neighbourhoods, foreign workers are a high proportion, even a majority of the population, but they are generally excluded from political decision-making at both local and national levels (Layton-Henry, 1990:17–18).

Indeed, he goes on to write that 'immigration has rendered obsolete accepted definitions of membership in, and citizenship of, a modern state' (Layton-Henry, 1990:17–18&186). From the point of view of the analyst, these accepted definitions may well have become obsolete, as evidenced in the increasingly popular concept of a 'continuum' of citizenship rights, according to which citizenship is no longer seen in all-or-nothing terms, but rather as fitting into a more fluid structure within which different individuals hold different rights according to their residence status in any one state (e.g. illegal immigrants/temporary visitors/permanent foreign residents/full 'citizens').

That such a structure does reflect the social and political reality in Western Europe today is well documented elsewhere.[13] What is particularly salient to the multicultural model is the fact that the boundaries separating one membership status from another tend to coincide with ethnic or cultural boundaries. This is because the different 'frontiers' of citizenship affect immigrants and their offspring rather than native-born members of the 'indigenous' population (as opposed, for example, to a situation in which rights are differentiated according to social class or gender). The very fact that it is immigrant minority populations who bear the brunt of this differentiation leads one to question whether traditional notions of citizenship have, in fact, been rendered obsolete.

As argued by Gellner, modern industrial society will have to respect cultural differences where they persist, 'provided that they are superficial and do not engender genuine barriers between people, in which case the barriers, not the cultures, constitute a

---

[13] See, for example: Hammar, 1990; Layton-Henry, 1990; Baubock, 1992.

grave problem' (Gellner, 1983:121). Rainer Baubock notes that the inequalities inherent in this structure can be minimized only by equalizing the rights attached to each status, or by modifying the boundaries between categories such that upward mobility from one position to another is made easier (Baubock, 1992:73–114).

To the extent that integration policies have concentrated on strengthening immigrant minorities' social and economic rights and opportunities, West European states seem to have favoured the equalization of rights. These efforts have not been matched in the sphere of political rights, however, and this is seen by many observers, and by minority members themselves, as a very significant obstacle in the way of immigrant minorities' full social, economic and political incorporation (Hammar, 1990; Layton-Henry, 1990).

Moves have also been made to ease immigrants' transition from one status to another, for instance, through 'amnesty' programmes for illegal immigrants, a shortening of the time period necessary to achieve permanent residence status, and a relaxation of naturalization laws and procedures. However, in this respect, the situation varies considerably from one country to another. In the United Kingdom, for example, the majority of immigrants entered as British subjects with full citizenship rights. The problems here, then, stem less from *de jure* differentiation of rights than from the problems that minorities have experienced in exercising those rights (most notably as a result of discrimination). As already noted, in Germany the formal 'frontiers' of citizenship are particularly strong, and transition from one status to another is, in relative terms, very difficult. This is despite recent moves to lower the administrative barriers to naturalization.[14]

The citizenship question is still a very thorny issue in most countries, particularly in the context of political rights, naturalization and dual citizenship. This indicates not only that traditional

[14] For an informed discussion of citizenship rights in different countries of Western Europe in the context of immigration, see Hammar, 1990.

concepts of citizenship or membership have become more difficult to apply, but also that no clear alternative structure has yet been found to take their place. As Baubock asks,

How can equality and universality of rights be maintained in societies open for immigration and internal multiculturalism? The formidable problems involved in this openness remind us how strongly the Western liberal concept of citizenship has been rooted in national closure, in the double meaning of limited access from outside and cultural homogenisation inside (Baubock, 1992:7).

These deeper tensions are evident in the interaction of immigration and integration policies in Western Europe. It is argued in the Council of Europe report on community relations that integration of immigrant and ethnic minorities can only be achieved on the basis of 'open, welcoming and tolerant attitudes' so that immigrant minorities are 'made to feel that they are accepted as an integral part of society'; and it is asserted that integration is not about migrants as a 'separate and problematic group', but rather about the interaction of different communities which go to make up society as a whole (Council of Europe, 1991:25). And yet there is a parallel and near-universal maxim governing policy throughout Western Europe holding that immigrant minorities' integration can only be achieved if all further immigration is restricted. This argument could be seen to imply that past immigration, particularly from outside Europe, constituted a deviation from the norm which can only be corrected by closing the borders once again and concentrating on the integration of those who have settled. Looked at in this way, immigrant or ethnic minority communities may indeed be seen as a 'separate and problematic' group. Moreover, a closed and decidedly unwelcoming attitude to further immigrants is unlikely to be easily reconciled with an 'open' and 'welcoming' attitude to those who have already settled.

Despite efforts to speed immigrant and ethnic minorities' integration in terms of improving their social, economic and (to a lesser extent) political rights and opportunities, it is not at all clear that

West European society is reconciled to the cultural and ethnic diversity which the last few decades of immigration have brought about. Indeed, at a time of considerable economic and political uncertainty, and at a time when the traditional frontiers of the state are being eroded by a range of transnational and global economic, political and social forces (including migration), there is a potential for society in Western Europe to turn increasingly to negative symbols of identity (i.e. to base their identity on opposition to the identities of others). There is also a potential for states to rely more and more on the (always important) negative bases of legitimation, that is, what society must be protected from. In this context, immigration, or the threat of it, may perform a dual role. It may provide an immediate target community of 'significant others' (Smith, 1992:75) upon which to base a communal identity; and it may provide the state or wider grouping of states with a new concept of what is threatening (Garcia, 1992:12) and needing to be controlled, perhaps replacing the threat formerly represented by the communist Eastern bloc. As Mary Douglas observes, 'Any tribal culture selects this and that danger to fear and sets up demarcation lines to control it. It allows people to live contentedly with a hundred other dangers which ought to terrify them out of their wits' (Douglas, 1975:246–7). If clear demarcation lines are set up against the immigrant, there may be little hope of Western Europe achieving the kind of multicultural society which its proponents usually have in mind.

3

Immigration control and migration policy

Policies on the control and regulation of immigration in Western Europe have varied as much as those on immigrant settlement and integration. Although it is possible to chart common shifts in policy during the latter half of this century – at least among the major immigration countries of northwestern Europe – the particular form, dynamics and rationale of in-migration has differed considerably from one state to the next.[1] Nevertheless, a visible element linking all the policies pursued in the region throughout this period has been that of a largely reactive, defensive and short-term approach to migration. The labour recruitment policies pursued by a number of states in northwestern Europe from the 1950s to the early 1970s, for example, represented short-term responses to immediate pressures in the labour market. The near-universal halt on labour immigration which followed in the early to mid-1970s came about in reaction to an emerging recognition of, and anxiety about, the social, cultural and political implications of the immigration which had already taken place, and in response to the economic downturn which followed the 1973 oil crisis. In general, the policies pursued during the 1970s and 1980s – including those to restrict or regulate family immigration, efforts to encourage return migration, or, alternatively, the integration of those who had settled – developed essentially in reaction to the policies which had been pursued during the preceding decades.

[1] For a discussion of the development of migration policies in Western Europe after the Second World War, see Collinson, 1993; and Kubat, ed., 1993.

If Europe is indeed on the threshold of a new migration 'crisis', it is salient to examine the current development of migration policy in Western Europe, and assess in particular whether the now well-established pattern of 'muddling through' (Kubat, 1993:xi) continues to dominate, or whether – for perhaps the first time – policy appears set to develop in the forward-looking way which current challenges necessitate.

Policy developments up to 1989

Partly as a consequence of their reactive stance to migration matters, receiving states' control over the migration process has always been incomplete. However, it has never been entirely lacking. Thus, during the 1970s and 1980s, immigration was ever-present on the political agenda, but there was little sense of crisis, for although the 1973/4 labour recruitment halt failed to bring about an actual freeze on immigration, it did have a substantial stabilizing effect on Western Europe's immigrant population, at least in terms of overall numbers.[2] Attention turned progressively towards questions related to the legal, social, economic and political problems (real or perceived) associated with Western Europe's new immigrant minority populations. This was reflected in the European Community and Council of Europe initiatives of the time, which included the adoption of an EC Action Programme in Favour of Migrant Workers (1974), and the formulation of a European Convention on the Legal Status of Migrant Workers (1977).[3]

Nevertheless, receiving states remained on the defensive vis-à-vis continuing immigration, and very little emerged in terms of positive or forward-looking policies in the migration field after the 1973/4 recruitment halt. What policy-makers stressed above all was the need to control and regulate immigration, and, as a result,

[2] Note, for example, that the legally resident foreign population of Germany increased by only 5.7% between 1974 and 1984 (OECD, 1986). Note, however, that the impact of new immigration controls differed from one immigrant group to another (see Collinson, 1993:87).
[3] For a discussion of this Convention, see Plender, 1988.

immigration policy in Western Europe became synonymous with immigration restriction and control. As noted in the previous chapter, the emphasis was placed on putting right the 'mistakes' of the past: to integrate those immigrants who had settled, and to begin closing the doors to any further immigration, at least from outside Europe. This stance was sustained not only on the basis of social, cultural and political concerns, but also on the basis of economic considerations, as unemployment had started to emerge as a persistent problem for all the West European economies.

Unemployment did not, however, impede moves to liberalize controls on the movement of persons within the European Community. While economic and political concerns seemed to be calling for the closing-off of some migration channels, they were simultaneously motivating an expansion of others. As observed by Emmerij, the pattern which emerged in the migration field mirrored that in the global product market, namely 'a combination of globalisation and regionalisation, of outward-orientation and inward-orientation, of free movement and barriers, analogous to the combination of free trade and protectionism' (Emmerij, 1991:9).

The Single European Act (SEA), when ratified in 1987, introduced a new article into the EEC Treaty of Rome (Article 8a) stipulating that an internal market be established by 31 December 1992 comprising 'an area without internal frontiers in which the free movement of goods, *persons*, services, and capital is ensured' (emphasis added).[4] This was a turning-point in the migration policy regimes of the member states of the European Community. Not only did it represent a changing environment for the movement of persons within the Community, but it also implied closer cooperation among the member states on matters connected with migration into the Community from outside, since, with the abolition of internal borders, the external borders of each member state were effectively to become the external borders for the Community

[4] Note that in the light of restrictions on the movement, residence and establishment rights of third-country nationals in the European Community, 'persons' in the context of Article 8a should be interpreted as referring to EC citizens.

as a whole. As expressed in the declaration accompanying the SEA, 'in order to promote the free movement of persons, the Member States shall cooperate ... as regards the entry, movement and residence of nationals of third countries'. The same reasoning applied to the Schengen Agreement on the gradual abolition of controls at the common frontiers, signed between France, Germany and the Benelux countries in 1985.[5]

It was clear that, in both the EC and the Schengen grouping, the abolition of internal frontiers would prove a complex process, particularly in respect of controls on the movement of persons. Not only were states still guarding their national sovereignty in such matters, but it was evident then (as now) that many of the interests and concerns of the member states did not entirely coincide. The EC member states resisted pressure from the Commission to acknowledge Community competence in the area and thus opted to continue with the intergovernmental approach. Matters connected directly with migration were to be dealt with primarily by a group of ministers and senior civil servants responsible for immigration – the Ad Hoc Group on Immigration – which was set up in 1986. As other intergovernmental groups were also involved in the negotiations associated with the completion of the internal market (including the European Political Cooperation and Trevi Groups), the European Council decided to establish a Group of Coordinators in 1988 to speed up the work needed to meet the 1992

[5] This was motivated by a desire to make swifter progress than was being made among the EC-12. Note that the original five signatory states were subsequently joined by Italy (1990), Spain (1991), Portugal (1991), and Greece (1992). The Schengen Group signed an Implementing Convention in 1990, which sets out a wide range of provisions for the abolition of internal borders. To a a great extent, the Schengen initiative has been looked upon positively by the Commission and other EC member states, as it has been seen as a 'laboratory' for developments planned to take place within the EC itself. The founding member states of Schengen are expected to suppress their internal borders by the end of 1993 or beginning of 1994. The External Borders Convention, due to be signed by the EC-12, is modelled on the provisions affecting movement of persons of the Schengen Implementing Convention. See Collinson, Miall and Michalski, 1993:26–38. For a full discussion of the Schengen grouping, see Meijers et al., 1991.

deadline and to ensure coherence among the different bodies.[6]

It is important to stress that moves to cooperate on matters connected with migration were instigated almost exclusively by efforts to complete the internal market. This was reflected in the so-called 'Palma Document', drawn up by the Group of Coordinators and issued by the European Council in 1989, which listed problems to be solved if the free movement of persons in the Community was to be achieved. The list placed the emphasis on problems linked directly to physical controls at the internal and external borders, leaving aside for future discussion the development of a common immigration policy and common agreements on the status of third-country nationals. Thus, the EC-92 process was to bring about the coordination of traditional national control measures at the EC level. It did not imply a significant change of course in the immigration policies of the member states. Indeed, if anything it implied a further entrenchment and expansion of restrictive policies controlling migration from outside the Community, as the strongest – not the weakest – external borders were to provide the common denominator.

Policy developments since 1989

The fact that the Palma Document was felt necessary reflected the complexity of the negotiations over the movement of persons, and a certain anxiety over the (disputed) need to meet the 1992 deadline. This deadline (which has, in fact, been missed) would have been difficult to meet at the best of times, but was made even more so by the events which took place in Eastern/Central Europe in 1989. As noted in Chapter 1, the euphoria which accompanied the collapse of the Eastern bloc soon gave way to a growing sense of anxiety which focused increasingly on migration. Worries began to be voiced over the apparent threat of mass uncontrolled East–West

[6] Note that the Maastricht treaty further institutionalizes the intergovernmental approach, containing only limited provision for the transfer of competence in immigration matters to the Community (Article 100.c: common visa policy), and listing almost all other matters relating to migration under Title IV (Cooperation in the Fields of Justice and Home Affairs).

migration, worries which only added to what was already a growing anxiety over rising numbers of asylum-seekers and illegal immigrants from the 'South'. The prospect of the abolition of internal border controls meant that concerns which might otherwise have remained specific to the countries most directly affected came to be seen as the concerns of the Community as a whole.

Developments during the early 1990s have demonstrated both a new sense of urgency in policy formulation, and a shift in emphasis as the agenda has been widened to take account of broader concerns connected with the build-up of external migration pressures and increasing inflows of asylum-seekers and undocumented immigrants. This shift has not, however, taken place in an environment entirely conducive to the development of coherent and sustainable policies. The collapse of the Eastern bloc has given rise to considerable confusion regarding West European policies towards Eastern/Central Europe and the former Soviet Union. New strategies have had to be developed rapidly and in new directions to tackle an enormous range of problems – many seemingly intractable – connected with political and economic reform and transformation in the region. The emerging sense of vulnerability, and the inability to respond effectively to a number of actual or potential economic and political developments in Eastern/Central Europe and other parts of the world, have given rise to a crisis of confidence which has been exacerbated by developments within Western Europe itself, most notably the economic recession and a serious loss of momentum in the EC integration process (Papademetriou, 1993). The upshot has been considerable apprehension about the future economic and political security and cohesion of Western Europe. It is in this reactive, defensive and muddled political and economic context that the migration issue has moved up the political agenda in Western Europe during the early part of 1990s.

The new policy 'regime'
The increasing prominence of the migration issue in the European context is reflected in the recent explosion of multilateral activities

in the field. According to one observer, there are now 15 multilateral fora dealing with migration problems in Europe, as compared with five in the mid-1980s (Widgren, 1993). Extending beyond the EC, Schengen and EFTA groupings,[7] these include the activities of organizations with a well-established role in the field (such as the Council of Europe, the International Organisation for Migration, the United Nations High Commission for Refugees, and the OECD), others which have only recently started examining the issue, such as the Conference on Security and Cooperation in Europe (CSCE), and new groupings which have emerged to tackle specific aspects of the phenomenon.[8] Activity at the multilateral level reflects four central features of the post-1989 policy 'regime' as it is developing in Western Europe.

First, the *widened agenda*, as reflected in the diversity of international institutions now involved in the issue. In the EC context, a 'Work Programme' submitted by the Ad Hoc Group on Immigration to the European Council in Maastricht in December 1991 reveals a broadening of policy concerns beyond those linked directly to the harmonization of border arrangements, listing a number of areas of migration and asylum policy requiring further work (Ad Hoc Group on Immigration, 1991). Five main categories are listed under the heading of migration policy: the harmonization of admission policies; a common approach to the problem of

[7] Note that the EFTA states are set to become more fully integrated with the regime governing migration policy and the movement of persons in the EC. This would be an inevitable consequence of the establishment of the European Economic Area (involving the relaxation of common frontiers and rights of free movement for nationals of the signatory third countries), and of these states joining the EC (according to the principle of *acquis communautaire*). See Collinson, Miall and Michalski, 1993:33–4.

[8] These include the so-called 'Vienna Group' emanating from the Council of Europe Ministerial Conference on the Movement of Persons from Central and Eastern European Countries which was held in Vienna in January 1991; and the 'Berlin Group' created by the Berlin Conference on European Cooperation to Prevent Uncontrolled Migration convened in October 1991, attended by the EC and EFTA states plus the Soviet Union and Central/East European states (subsequently the 'Budapest' grouping following a second conference in Budapest in February 1993).

illegal immigration; policy on the migration of labour; the situation of third-country nationals; and migration policy 'in the broad meaning of the term', including action to tackle external migration pressures.

A second (linked) feature is a new emphasis on *joint action* at the international level. This is also indicated in the Ad Hoc Group's Work Programme, where it is stated that:

> The pressure of immigration in most Member States has increased significantly in recent years. The conviction that, confronted with these developments, a strictly national policy could not provide an adequate response has been consistently gaining ground ... [and on] that basis, it would appear advisable to define a common answer to the question of how this immigration pressure can be accommodated ... [The] aim is to make the problems manageable for the entire Community. This will require ... an extended form of cooperation among Member States (Ad Hoc Group on Immigration, 1991:13).

Indeed, recent developments show a concern among West European states to establish a European policy regime extending beyond the boundaries of the Schengen, Community or EFTA groupings. To some extent, responsibility for developing this regime is seen to fall to institutions such as the Council of Europe and CSCE in which representation already extends to Eastern/Central Europe and the former Soviet Union. However, West European states (and, in particular, the EC member states) have been concerned to introduce a stronger regime than could be achieved through cooperation in other existing intergovernmental fora, at least as regards controlling migratory flows across their external borders.

The first states to be involved in this process were those already associated with the European Community on the basis of the Europe Agreements (the Visegrad states – the Czech and Slovak Republics, Poland and Hungary), and others identified as primary sources of 'unwanted' migration into Western Europe, such as Romania. The Europe Agreements themselves reflect the ambiguous position of the East/Central European countries regarding the movement of persons and control over migration. These states are essentially migrant-sending countries in respect of the EC, and thus the Europe Agreements – while containing provisions related to these countries' association with EC labour markets (provisions allowing for movement for the purposes of self-employment) – contain only very weak provisions for those seeking employment.[9] However, the states in question are now also seen as potentially important partners for controlling migration, whether it be the migration of their own nationals, or that of migrants in transit from other countries further east or from other parts of the world. Indeed, the Visegrad states in particular are now experiencing significant levels of undocumented immigration and asylum in-flows, much of which is potentially destined for Western Europe.[10]

This is reflected in the so-called 'Berlin process' set in motion by the Intergovernmental Conference on European Cooperation to Prevent Uncontrolled Migration convened in Berlin in October 1991. The conference was attended by the EC and EFTA states plus the Soviet Union and East/Central European states, and led to the adoption of a list of policy recommendations by all the states involved at a second intergovernmental conference in Budapest in February 1993. These included recommendations on 'the

[9] In contrast to the free movement provisions for states joining the European Economic Area. Note that the Europe agreements contain no right of access for workers from the Association countries, but (i) protection from discrimination as regards working conditions, remuneration or dismissal when workers are lawfully employed in the EC; and (ii) access to the labour market for legally resident spouses and children of a legally employed worker for the duration of the worker's authorized employment. See Guild, 1992.

[10] The Council of Europe's 1992 Recommendation on Migratory Flows in Czechoslovakia, Hungary and Poland notes the importance of 'migratory waves flowing into these three countries, underscoring the fact that these central European states are both emigration and immigration countries'. Parliamentary Assembly of the Council of Europe, Recommendation 1188 (1992). According to statements made at a CSCE Seminar on Migration (Warsaw, April 1992), Poland was host to an estimated 290,000 irregular immigrants, primarily from the former Soviet Union, Romania and Bulgaria. Hungary received over 100,000 asylum-seekers during the period 1988–92.

criminalisation of smuggling of illegal migrants', and 'procedures and standards for the improvement of control at the border' (Berlin Working Party, 1993). The importance attached to the role of existing or potential migrant-sending states is also reflected in the recent adoption of a number of 'readmission agreements' between West and East/Central European states, including that between the Schengen states and Poland which imposes a mutual obligation on each party to 'readmit to its territory, on the request of any other party, without formalities, any person who does not fulfil (or who no longer fulfils) the conditions for entry or residence prevailing on the territory of the requesting party' (Art.1[1]).[11]

The new structure of cooperative arrangements between the West European states and those of Eastern/Central Europe (and to a lesser extent, states to the south) clearly reflects, third, an overbearing *defensiveness* on the part of Western Europe. Both the Berlin process and the readmission agreements are significant in this respect in that they represent efforts to externalize migration control in the aim of creating a 'buffer zone' protecting the external borders of the European Community and EFTA. This zone will be all the more effective because the intensification of immigration pressures on the Central European states, combined with barriers to movement westwards, is forcing these states to develop their own immigration controls similar to those operating in Western Europe (Collinson, Miall and Michalski, 1993:34–8).[12]

This defensiveness is also reflected in policy developments within the Community itself. Despite the broadened policy agenda and a willingness to discuss wider aspects of the migration issue, priority in the formulation of concrete cooperative arrangements has been given to the enhancement of restrictive control and enforcement mechanisms. This was indicated by the London meeting of EC Ministers Responsible for Immigration in November/December 1992 (as discussed in Chapter 4), of which the most important outcome was the adoption of Resolutions and Conclu-

[11] See O'Keefe, 1993:195.
[12] Note, for example, a readmission agreement signed between Poland and Slovakia on 9 July 1993. See *Migration News Sheet*, August 1993.

sions designed to restrict access to asylum systems in the Community (Ad Hoc Group on Immigration, 1992). It was also indicated in the agenda at Copenhagen in June 1993, which included as one of only three Resolutions that 'concerning checks on and expulsion of third-country nationals residing or working without authorisation' (Ad Hoc Group on Immigration, 1993).[13]

To some extent, the emphasis on restrictive measures is symptomatic of a fourth feature of the present policy regime, that being a certain *confusion and overload* associated with the broadened policy agenda. At the trans-European level, this is marked by considerable institutional crowding caused by a failure to synchronize and streamline the activities of the different multilateral organizations involved. This in turn derives from the complexity of the issues and, importantly, from the failure of governments to think out and agree on a comprehensive plan of action with clear guidelines for implementation (particularly in respect of action to tackle the root causes of migration, as discussed below). At the EC level, it is reflected in the form of cooperative agreements now being negotiated. Given the slow progress being made within the framework of formal treaty arrangements,[14] the emphasis has

[13] Ministers also reached a Resolution on harmonization of national policies on family reunification, and a Resolution on certain common guidelines as regards the admission of particularly vulnerable groups of persons from the former Yugoslavia. The provisions of the former are very vague as member states could not agree to common policies on family reunification and have come under attack from a recent European Parliament Resolution on European immigration policy for being 'likely not to respect private life' (15 July 1993). The provisions included in the latter indicate a restrictive stance towards temporary protection for victims of civil war.

[14] Note that the processes set in motion by the Single European Act have run into a variety of problems including the failure to secure the signature of the Convention on the Crossing of External Borders (owing to a disagreement between the UK and Spain over the status of Gibraltar), and the failure to reach agreement on what 'an area without internal frontiers' actually entails (the UK government's continued insistence that limited documentation checks on persons entering the country from another member state are compatible with Article 8a of the SEA – a view shared by the governments of Ireland and Denmark – conflicts with the position taken by the Schengen states and by the European Commission, as set out in the Commission's May 1992 document on the Abolition of Border Controls).

shifted from the formulation of treaties to that of 'Resolutions', 'Conclusions' and 'Recommendations' - flexible agreements with political, but no legal, force.

In short, developments since 1989 reveal an interest within Western Europe in formulating more comprehensive approaches to migration at the international level, including action to tackle the root causes of migration, and greater cooperation with migrant-sending countries in Eastern/Central Europe and further afield. However, progress in this respect is seriously hampered by confusion *vis-à-vis* the objectives and expected outcome of wider policies or strategies proposed, as well as the lack of political will behind them; and by the defensive and essentially reactive stance of the West European states. Thus, the emerging pattern of migration policy in Western Europe is one in which increasing stress is placed on restrictive control mechanisms. This defensiveness is strengthened by a growing sense of vulnerability to external migration pressures, and by economic recession and political malaise at home.

The limitations of current policy

Despite efforts to introduce stricter controls and restrictions on entry, immigration into Western Europe continues, whether it be in the form of unauthorized immigration (as dominates in Southern Europe), asylum inflows, particularly into Germany,[15] authorized inflows of workers (predominantly highly skilled workers and professionals), family immigration, involving family members of both the 'indigenous' population and settled immigrants, or 'national' flows, for example, ethnic Germans from Central/Eastern Europe. What factors, therefore, militate against the West European states gaining the desired control over the phenomenon?

[15] Note that Germany has received over half the total number of asylum applications lodged in the European Community since 1989.

The 'market forces' of migration: 'pull' factors

As reflected in recent calls to tackle external migration pressures, many of the causes of current migration are to be found in the sending countries or regions. External migration pressures include economic stagnation or decline, rising unemployment, political instability and population growth. Indeed, the intensity of these pressures, coupled with the introduction of restrictive immigration policies and a concomitant increase in unauthorized immigration into Western Europe, has caused some to argue that current migration flows are caused almost exclusively by external 'push' factors. Although the current focus on external migration pressures may be seen as an essentially positive development, on the negative side it has given rise to a certain sense of impotence in the face of continuing immigration, and has diverted attention away from a number of internal economic, social, and political factors which create a significant 'pull' on immigration from outside.

The most visible pull factor derives from the fact that almost all West European states are now host to substantial immigrant or immigrant-origin populations, and thus important immigration channels have already been opened up. Since the early 1970s, efforts have been made to close off the immigration channels of the past, but they nevertheless remain partially open, at least for (restricted) family immigration, and – in some cases – for unauthorized immigration (which frequently follows the path of authorized immigration). It is also important to note that as a function of increasing international travel and expanding international networks of communication, family migration which is independent of past labour or other immigration flows (e.g. the migration of 'indigenous' residents' foreign spouses) has become an important and persistent component of migration into, out of and within Western Europe.[16]

Yet there are additional factors creating a 'pull' which, although less visible, may be more significant. These derive from labour

---

[16] For statistics on family migration to and from the UK, see Office of Population Censuses and Surveys (OPCS), 1993.

market structures in Western Europe which imply a continuing dependence on immigrant workers,[17] despite persistent unemployment and the present economic downturn. Current demand can be identified at both the upper and lower levels of Western Europe's labour markets. This reflects in part their progressive segmentation, which is in turn linked to difficulties in overcoming rigidities and effecting economic restructuring.

At the upper end, an increasing demand for, and international mobility of, highly skilled professional, managerial and technical workers reflects two factors: first, the globalization of the world economy and its labour market, implying a new international division of labour and an internationalization of companies and human resources; and, second, a failure to match labour supply with demand as labour markets have become increasingly diversified (in particular through insufficient or inadequate training and education of indigenous workers to suit new and rapidly changing technologies). The international movement of highly skilled workers is now a growing feature in Western Europe, both within the region, and into the region from outside.[18] For example, the number of migrants entering the UK for the purposes of professional or managerial employment has almost doubled since 1982 (Office of Population Censuses and Surveys, 1993:xi).[19]

The movement of highly skilled workers is, however, relatively easy to regulate, and is generally not viewed as a problem for the receiving countries; instead, it is usually seen as a problem for the sending countries, in terms of 'brain-drain'. Moreover, the greatest

[17] Demographic and economic developments combined may imply an increasing dependence (linked to ageing of the population and a growing 'demographic deficit'). See, for example, Straubhaar and Zimmerman, 1992. However, this view is challenged by some analysts. See, for example, Coleman, 1992.

[18] For a discussion of the growing importance of this category of migration, see Salt, 1991 and 1993.

[19] The inflow of professional and managerial workers into the UK increased from 43,700 in 1982 to 80,500 in 1991, although this has been balanced by outflows. In terms of gross flows, this category of migration is as significant as family migration, and more significant than asylum flows for the UK. Office of Population Censuses and Surveys, 1993.

proportion of this migration is temporary or transient. It is, rather, the persistence of the immigration of workers to fill jobs at the lower end of the labour market spectrum which is seen as a primary problem in Western Europe, especially that part of the immigration which is unauthorized and thus uncontrolled.[20] At the lower end, a demand for foreign workers persists in marginal and relatively unregulated sectors of the economy which depend on a cheap and exploitable workforce to remain competitive; this is particularly the case in labour-sensitive service industries (e.g. hotel and catering), certain marginal labour-intensive industries (e.g. textiles and clothing), and agriculture. Unauthorized immigrant workers are particularly appealing in these sectors because they are generally cheaper than both legal immigrants and indigenous workers, and are 'totally flexible' with regard to wage rates and working conditions. As is particularly evident in Southern Europe, unauthorized immigration and a strong informal economy tend to go hand-in-hand, the one supporting and reinforcing the other. The number of unauthorized immigrants residing in the European Community can only be guessed at, although most estimates range around the two million mark.[21]

In short, an important motor behind current 'economic' migration into Western Europe derives from a failure to regulate or restructure low-wage labour markets and to tackle the problem of regional or sectoral labour deficits. Thus it can be argued that an important shortcoming of current policy initiatives in the migration field is a failure to reconcile in any comprehensive way the stated aims of immigration policy (restriction and control) with the reality of continuing demand or pull within Western Europe itself. It is worth noting, for example, that the recent Resolution of EC Immigration Ministers 'concerning checks on and expulsion of third country nationals residing or working without authorisation'

[20] Note that 'labour migration' includes smaller, more regulated, movements of seasonal or frontier workers, domestic servants, short-term casual workers (e.g. Australians and New Zealanders working for short periods in the UK), and small numbers of contract labour migrants.
[21] See, for example, Salt, 1991:15.

makes no reference to labour market policies which could influence levels of undocumented immigration. Instead, the Resolution simply notes the need for direct measures 'to combat the employment of those known to have entered or remained illegally or those whose immigration status does not allow them to work' (Ad Hoc Group on Immigration, 1993:3).

Yet if one assumes that the eradication of both 'push' factors (discussed below) and 'pull' or demand factors is only likely to be achieved in the longer term (if at all), what are the prospects for control in the short to medium term? As argued by John Salt, undocumented labour migrants are an important group whose numbers seem likely to rise as migrant-receiving countries adopt a more restrictive approach because 'increasingly desperate migrants will attempt to circumvent tightened entry control procedures' (Salt, 1993:3).

The limits of immigration controls

'Economic' migration into Western Europe has developed its own dynamic, supported by a range of economic, political and social pressures which are both internal and external to the receiving states. Indeed, if the past few decades of immigration indicate anything, it is that immigration is always far more difficult to stop than to start. At a time when pressure is mounting for the introduction of ever more restrictive controls, it is important to consider the practical and political limits of immigration controls in the democratic states of Western Europe.

The most obvious practical limitation is that of the difficulty in policing external borders. Explicit external controls, such as restrictive visa regimes, and documentation checks at the main entry points, of course have an effect in restricting entry through formal channels. This effect is further strengthened by more implicit forms of external control, such as the arbitrary, discriminatory or 'erratic' application of immigration laws or rules by immigration officials. Unauthorized immigration may be considerably restricted through the now increasingly important forms of 'externalized' controls, including the imposition of penalties for carriers transporting foreigners without the requisite documentation, and the creation of 'buffer zones' by means of readmission agreements with third countries of emigration or transit. Yet such controls can never be expected to be entirely successful, and thus the policing of borders will continue to be important.[22] Long land-borders and coastlines cannot be policed much more effectively than at present, however, without considerable economic costs. Moreover, the practical obstacles are so great that the pay-off in terms of increased detection and expulsion is unlikely to be proportional to the additional financial (and political) burden that such stepped-up policing would entail (Brochmann, 1992).

Immigration controls, however, do not operate only at the external borders. Because external borders are so difficult to police, and because a substantial proportion of unregulated immigration takes place initially through legal entry channels (e.g. immigrants who enter on short-term visas and subsequently overstay), most countries also rely on forms of internal control which, like external controls, are both explicit and implicit in nature. Explicit controls include the use of identity cards or other proof of legality to control access to a range of public and private services, such as housing, health-care, banking services, and social benefits; 'random' stop-and-search documentation checks; and employer sanctions, i.e. the fining of companies found to be employing unauthorized workers. More hidden control mechanisms may also be in operation, particularly in countries, such as the United Kingdom, where explicit internal controls are not formalized. Networks of 'devolved controllers', including teachers and housing officials, as well as unofficial informers, may play as important a role in detecting unauthorized immigrants as the police or immigration officials (Owers, 1993).

Here too, however, the practical obstacles and financial costs associated with stepping up controls are considerable. Italy, for

---

[22] Note the emphasis placed on direct border controls in the Recommendation drawn up by the Berlin Working Party for the Budapest Intergovernmental Conference to Prevent Uncontrolled Migration in February 1993, at which most European states were represented. See Berlin Working Party, 1993.

example, has had little success in stemming the continuing influx of unauthorized immigrants, despite having a regime of identity cards and employer sanctions. Perhaps more important, however, are the political costs which would be associated with an intensified system of internal surveillance. First, such measures, particularly those most open to arbitrary or discriminatory application (e.g. stop-and-search policies), would almost certainly impinge most on immigrant or ethnic minority groups, thereby fuelling social and political frictions which are already a serious and growing cause for concern in Western Europe.[23] Second, one is led to consider whether intensifying such forms of control might come at the price of civil liberties for all (Gibney, 1988:xiii). A truly effective system of internal immigration control might require an extension of state powers so great as to threaten the very constitutional foundations of Western Europe's liberal democracies. Such considerations have to be balanced against the political costs associated with not expanding internal control systems.

The costs of the current restrictive regime
Despite its most obvious shortcomings, current policy can be seen to be basically rational and pragmatic: policy-makers can respond to growing public anxiety over immigration by attempting to restrict it, while – because restriction is imperfect – simultaneously remaining responsive to the economy, if only informally. However, this approach can only be sustained in the longer term at considerable political and economic cost.

Important political problems derive in the first place from a vicious spiral which almost inevitably results from an emphasis on restriction and control in conditions of continuing immigration – a spiral in which anxieties may be heightened rather than quelled. A

---

[23] Note the recent controversy in France surrounding the government's attempts to pass an amendment to the country's new immigration bill which would have allowed police to request identity papers if they notice 'any element other than racial affiliation' which causes them to suspect that person is a foreigner. See *The Times*, *The Independent* and *Le Monde*, 24 June 1993.

defensive and restrictive stance towards immigration either implicitly or explicitly defines immigration as a problem. The receiving society may thus be rendered more sensitive to the immigration which continues (and to that which has already taken place), at the same time as confidence is undermined in the (seemingly ineffective) controls in place. This in turn may create pressure for even more restrictive (and, very probably, equally ineffective) policies to be introduced. This seems to be the situation which has emerged in Western Europe over recent years, one which is all the more difficult because of the amount of attention now focused on the issue.

Associated political problems include the restriction of policy-makers' room for manoeuvre. The relationship between policy and public opinion is always very difficult to disentangle, but it seems that politicians could be digging themselves into something of a trap by emphasizing the need to restrict immigration further while at the same time failing to effect a significant reduction in immigration levels (Brochmann, 1992). Moreover, the widespread negative perception of immigration which is supported by this approach works against a recognition of the important economic and social value of immigration; encourages the linking of immigration with a number of economic and social problems of which immigration is not the primary cause (including unemployment); does serious damage to already weakened systems of refugee protection; and, importantly, reinforces hostile tendencies which not only endanger the security and integration of settled immigrants and minority groups, but may also have a detrimental effect on the social and political fabric of society as a whole (as is a particular concern in Germany at present). The need for vigilance to prevent such perceptions from taking root is all the greater at a time of economic downturn and rising unemployment, when immigrant minorities are already a vulnerable target for public discontent.

In terms of economic costs, both regulated and unregulated immigration may be allowing policy-makers to postpone difficult – and, at least in the short term, costly – decisions connected with economic restructuring and the regulation of labour markets

(Papademetriou, 1993). Moreover, as discussed in Chapter 5, current thinking allows policy-makers little room for working out how immigration, now and in the future, might best be regulated to the greatest benefit of the economies and societies of both sending and receiving states, including an evaluation of how certain forms of immigration might help ease inevitable, but painful, demographic and economic changes.

Lastly, in conditions of intensifying migration pressures and continuing immigration, the potential for restrictive measures to deflect immigration flows from one channel to another should be recognized. The dynamics of any immigration flow are very difficult to unravel, but it is possible that attempts to close off one channel (such as worker immigration) will lead to increased pressure on other channels (such as asylum).

The new concern with root causes

Difficulties in restricting immigration, coupled with a more generalized sense of vulnerability to external migration pressures, have encouraged policy-makers to consider the broader external roots of the phenomenon.[24] The EC member states are now talking of the 'external aspects' of migration policy, under which they list a diverse range of policy issues including

> the preservation of peace and the termination of armed conflicts; full respect for human rights; the creation of democratic societies and adequate social conditions; a liberal trade policy, which should improve economic conditions in the countries of emigration [and] co-ordination of action in the fields of foreign policy, [and] economic co-operation (European Council, 1992).

[24] In a UN context the idea of 'root causes' has been current since the early 1980s, principally in the context of refugee flows (see, for example, United Nations, 1985). However, it is only since the end of the Cold War that policy-makers in Western Europe have become explicitly concerned with the question in the context of both migration and refugee flows.

This should almost certainly be seen as an essentially positive development, for even a tentative move towards a greater recognition of the broader factors which give rise to migration is likely to result in a better understanding of the phenomenon, more informed discussion on the issue, and thus possibly more effective policies being developed, at least in the longer term. Yet when one considers more closely the way the root cause issue is approached at present, a number of problems come to light.

The most important reservations derive from the fact that the new concern with root causes is founded in the same defensive thinking which is simultaneously encouraging greater emphasis on direct immigration restrictions and controls. Action to tackle the root causes is treated as another 'solution' to *the* migration 'problem', and is therefore as reactive in its basis as action to strengthen immigration controls. The EC's Declaration on Principles Governing External Aspects of Migration Policy issued at the Edinburgh European Council in December 1992, for example, was inspired by the recognition that 'a number of different factors ... [are] important for the reduction of migratory movements into the Member States' (European Council, 1992:42). A closer look at the issue leads one to question whether a 'root-cause' strategy can be sustained if it is predicated almost exclusively on an interest in stopping or preventing migration.

First, it would appear that discussions on the issue involve a degree of self-delusion. Although there are some important policy areas where there is obvious and immediate potential for constructive action (in particular, encouraging respect for human rights and supporting the development of democratic institutions in existing or potential sending countries), experience indicates that here progress is likely to be slow and uncertain. In other areas – such as measures to prevent or resolve conflicts and to improve social and economic conditions in the countries of emigration – the prospects for any substantial results look extremely faint (at least in the short term), even if there is the political will to see such measures implemented. Developments in the former Yugoslavia have highlighted the problems that will almost certainly beset any efforts to prevent or resolve complex conflicts of the kind which are likely to dominate in the post-Cold War era; and to talk realistically of improving social and economic conditions in potential or existing migrant-sending regions begs fundamental questions relating to the structure of the international economy and, in particular, the structural economic imbalances which are at the root of much of today's migration.

Progress in such areas is likely to be achieved only in the longer term, and then only on the basis of clear and realistic objectives backed up by a level of political and economic commitment which has so far been largely lacking. Furthermore, one might question whether migration in itself – or the prospect of it – should be the starting-point for such action, since the 'external aspects of migration policy' are of central importance, irrespective of migration pressures and migration trends.

Moreover, the proposition that substantial improvements in economic and social conditions in sending regions will have a direct effect in reducing migratory flows betrays a misunderstanding of the migratory process. Migration is not simply a 'symptom' of straightforward 'pressures', such as relative poverty, overpopulation, or unemployment, but also a complex component of many forms of social, economic and political change. Indeed, economic development may itself constitute an important 'motor' for migration for several reasons. For example, it may provide more potential migrants with the resources which make migration possible; it may result in the disruption of local economic and social structures in potential migrant-sending regions; or it may expand economic and other channels of communication and intensify contact between potential or existing migrant-sending and migrant-receiving countries.[25] The relationship between migration and development is complex in the extreme, and understanding of it

[25] Note, for example, the findings of a recent research project carried out by a United States research commission, which identified a 'major paradox' in that 'the development process itself tends to stimulate migration in the short to medium term'. Commission for the Study of International Migration and Cooperative Economic Development, 1990:xxxvi.

still wholly inadequate for the planning of policy measures which are likely to have any immediate impact in terms of reducing levels of migration.

Lastly, discussions on root causes at the policy-making level indicate that migration is still treated as a single problem issue, despite a recognition of a broad range of forces which give rise to it. The root-cause approach has thus contributed little as yet to a conceptual disaggregation of the different types of migration. Indeed, the EC's Declaration on external migration policy even glosses over the fundamental distinction between forced and voluntary migration. Such an approach encourages the view that migration in general both *should* and *could* be stopped or prevented. But it could be argued that to stop or prevent *all* migration would amount to inhibiting any social, political or economic change – something which would be neither possible nor desirable (Zolberg et al., 1989:262). As noted in Chapter 1, migration takes many different forms in many different contexts, some of which may be highly disruptive, and some of which may be beneficial. A blanket approach to prevention misses the complexity of the phenomenon, and is thus unlikely to be adequately responsive to the questions and challenges raised by it.

In the context both of root causes and of immigration controls, a gap is opening up between migration as a continuing process and the rationale of receiving states' policies founded almost entirely on concepts of prevention and restriction. Thus migration policies in Western Europe would appear ill-equipped either to minimize the most disruptive effects and avoid the most disruptive forms, or to maximize the potential benefits of the migration which continues. Above all, the existing policy regime does not reflect a formal or open recognition that direct immigration controls rarely bring about full control over immigration, or that the 'management' of migration in a democracy is rarely or never synonymous with absolute control.

As discussed in Chapter 5, a more realistic policy regime does not necessarily imply a significant relaxation of immigration controls, nor a rejection of the root-cause approach. Many concerns surrounding current policy, such as those listed above, do not derive from the fact that immigration policy is restrictive or defensive. The problem is rather that all the emphasis is placed on restriction without any balance in terms of a positive or realistic stance on those forms of migration which are inevitable, least disruptive, or potentially beneficial. Effective management of migration requires a long-term view and an active stance which allows for the positive engagement of policy in what is an extremely complex and ultimately unavoidable feature of the modern world.

4

The asylum dilemma

In popular usage, the term 'refugee' has a broad meaning, signifying a person fleeing any one of a wide range of life-threatening conditions, including war, famine, natural disaster, oppression, persecution or massive human rights abuses. Such a conception captures the essentially humanitarian aspect of the refugee's predicament and the responses which this predicament calls for. However, the refugee phenomenon is at once humanitarian and political in nature. It is political not only by virtue of the conditions which generally cause it (e.g. war or persecution), but also by virtue of the political context within which it takes place – namely, a world divided into mutually exclusive states. Forced to flee abroad because they are unable to rely on their own state for protection and the maintenance of conditions necessary for their survival, refugees are 'genuine international outcasts, stateless, in the deep meaning of the term' (Zolberg et al., 1989:33).

Consequently, international systems of refugee protection reflect more than straightforward humanitarian concern. By creating an international legal and institutional framework within which refugees may find protection in a new state (refuge or asylum), or seek to regain the protection of the state of origin (repatriation), they represent efforts to find solutions to the particular juridical and political problems which refugees present to the international community. International refugee protection is designed essentially to protect persons in flight from states which fail in their basic duty of protection.

The 'international community', however, is not infinitely generous. A moral, legal or humanitarian obligation to offer protection to refugees, and the needs of refugees themselves, will, in practice, always be balanced against the political and economic interests and concerns of potential asylum states. It is for this reason that, when entering into international legal agreements or developing national refugee and asylum laws and policies, states have been careful to limit the scope of their obligations *vis-à-vis* the world's 'dispossessed'. For the same reason, the form and application of refugee assistance mechanisms have, in practice, been shaped considerably by both foreign and domestic political and economic interests. This is despite the fact that refugee policy – in contrast to migration policy – is governed by a relatively strict international legal regime.

The influence of political interest was particularly evident in Western refugee policy as it developed during the Cold War. As discussed below, Cold War political imperatives resulted in the West failing to respond in a comprehensive way to the refugee problems which developed during the second half of this century. The resulting 'policy deficit' was apparent relatively early on in the context of refugee movements in Africa and other parts of the world, but it was not until the mid-1980s that the strains began to show in the West itself. This marked the beginnings of a crisis in asylum policy which governments are still grappling with nearly a decade later.

The development of the current international refugee and asylum regime

The roots of today's international refugee regime go back to the interwar period when the League of Nations was called upon to respond to a whole series of refugee crises in Europe. At a time when the grip of nationalist and protectionist sentiment was becoming stronger and when states were attempting to reduce flows of immigrants, the League proved relatively limited in its ability to ensure refugee protection. Its success was restricted to legal rather than humanitarian assistance, and its activities were carried out in a largely *ad hoc* manner.

Nevertheless, the League's efforts were significant in that 'they distilled the concept of refugee from the European historical experience to date and made it concrete by creating a set of specialised agencies' (Zolberg et al., 1989:20). Most importantly, the League distinguished refugees as a particular group of migrants deserving international protection; it introduced a corollary obligation for states to respond to their needs; and it institutionalized the principle of asylum.

The League defined refugees in terms of specific ethnic groups or nationalities. This approach reflected pragmatism and a concern to limit the scope of international responsibility, as well as the more generalized emphasis on the claims of national groups which prevailed after the First World War. However, as Claudena Skran points out, this method of defining refugees lent itself to open political debates about which refugee groups should be assisted (Skran, 1992:20).

The late 1930s witnessed increasing pressure for a more universalist regime of refugee protection to be put in place. Such a regime would require the identification of criteria by which refugees as a distinct but universal category could be differentiated from other groups of foreigners and 'necessitous strangers'.[1] Early definitions focused on flight caused by 'political events' as opposed to economic conditions[2] – in a parallel to the current distinction between 'political' and 'economic' refugees in the media and popular discourse. Yet this criterion was quickly discounted as being too general. By the late 1940s refugee status had come to be conceived of as relating to individuals rather than groups,[3] and in essence a status resulting from a discord between an individual's

---

[1] A term used by Walzer, 1983:48.

[2] For example, that elaborated by the International Institute of International Law for its 1936 session. See Zolberg et al., 1989:20–21.

[3] Cf. moves away from an emphasis on national rights towards a system of universal human rights.

personal characteristics or convictions and the tenets of the political system in his or her country of origin. The hallmark of this discord was taken to be persecution or the threat of persecution by highly developed states (Shacknove, 1985). This conception captured not only the recent experience of refugees from Nazism, but also the new political concerns (and superior voting strength in the UN) of the Western Alliance, which was keen to accord priority to persons whose flight was motivated by anti-communist values (Hathaway, 1991:6–7). Moreover, the selection of 'persecution' as the key operational criterion was in keeping with the desire of the international community to make the status of refugee exceptional (Zolberg et al., 1989:25).

The central building blocks of today's international refugee regime were put in place by the United Nations in the early 1950s. In December 1949, the General Assembly adopted a resolution to create the office of the United Nations High Commissioner for Refugees (UNHCR), the Statute of which was adopted a year later. And in 1951, the Geneva Convention Relating to the Status of Refugees was adopted, an instrument which now forms the core of international refugee law.[4]

According to its Statute, the UNHCR was to have a strictly humanitarian and non-political function, providing international protection for refugees, seeking permanent solutions to the problem of refugees, and – according to Article 9 – engaging 'in such additional activities ... as the General Assembly may determine within the limits of the resources at her disposal'. Chapter II of the Statute begins by bringing within the UNHCR's competence refugees covered by various earlier treaties and arrangements. It then includes persons who are outside their country of origin as a result of events occurring before 1 January 1951 and who are unable or unwilling to avail themselves of its protection. And finally, the Statute extends to

[4] Note, however, that the United States did not accede to the 1951 Convention, although it was a major supporter of the UNHCR from the early 1950s. The USA opted for a more flexible conception of the 'refugee' which could be used as a more effective ideological weapon during the Cold War. See Loescher and Scanlan, 1986.

any other person who is outside the country of his nationality, or ... former habitual residence, because he has or had a well-founded fear of persecution by reason of his race, religion, nationality or political opinion and is unable or, because of such fear, is unwilling to avail himself of the protection of the government of the country of his nationality, or ... former habitual residence [emphasis added].[5]

The 1951 Convention adopts a refugee definition which differs little from that set out in the UNHCR Statute.[6] However, unlike the Statute, it limits application *only* to refugees who acquired such status as a result of events occurring before 1 January 1951, and includes an optional geographical limitation permitting states to restrict their obligations to refugees who have become such as a result of events occurring in Europe prior to the critical date. The Convention thus reflected states' concern to limit their obligations in respect of what was recognized to be a continuing problem.

Two major refugee crises arose outside Europe in the late 1940s which served as confirmation in this respect: that resulting from the partition of India (to which the international community did not respond), and that resulting from the formation of Israel (to which the United Nations responded by creating the UNRPR, later replaced by the UNRWA). It has been argued that, bearing in mind the lack of concern for the plight of refugees on the Indian sub-continent, the exceptional attention accorded to the Palestinians can be attributed less to humanitarian considerations than to the emergence of the Palestine problem as a prominent issue on the United Nations political agenda, and that the UNRWA was created largely as an instrument of US foreign policy (Zolberg et al., 1989:24).

[5] U.N.G.A. Res. 428(V), 14 December 1950.
[6] 1951 Convention Relating to the Status of Refugees (United Nations, *Treaty Series*, vol. 189, p. 137). The text of the Convention is reproduced in the UNHCR Handbook (UNHCR, 1988: Annex II).Note that the 1951 Convention definition adds 'membership of a social group' to the list of criteria which qualify as grounds for a well-founded fear of persecution. In practice, the 'social group' criterion overlaps significantly with the other four criteria listed in the Convention and in the UNHCR Statute.

In the face of strict policies governing entry into potential asylum states, refugee status may be seen as an 'entitlement or privilege' (Zolberg et al., 1989:1). Importantly, the 1951 Convention restricts states' sovereign control over the entry and exit of aliens by providing that states should refrain from expelling refugees lawfully in the territory of a contracting state, and by stipulating in Article 33 that 'No Contracting State shall expel or return a refugee in any manner whatsoever to the frontiers of territories where his life or freedom would be threatened on account of his race, nationality, political opinion or membership of a particular social group' (the principle of *non-refoulement*). Moreover, the Convention limits states' sovereign control over the treatment of refugees by setting out provisions that define the legal status of refugees and their rights and duties in the country of refuge.

On the other hand, the 1951 Convention implicitly supports the principle of state sovereignty by defining refugees as persons who have left their country of origin, the principle holding that the international community should not interfere in the internal affairs of a state.[7] Only when refugees have managed to escape their country of origin does the international community have a role to play. By defining refugees in this way, the Convention places all emphasis on the responsibilities of receiving countries as opposed to those of the sending countries. It is for this reason that the international refugee regime has had such difficulty in coming to grips with the problem of persons displaced within their country of origin (the numbers of which, worldwide, at least equal those of externally displaced); why little emphasis has been placed on causes and prevention; and why the refugee regime to date has worked in favour of refugees' external settlement (asylum), rather than return. Indeed, under the terms of the Convention, asylum is not only a measure of protection, but also a form of solution (Ogata,

[7] According to Chapter 1, Article 2.7 of the Charter of the United Nations. This principle is limited only by Chapter VII of the Charter (Action with Respect to Threats to the Peace, Breaches of the Peace, and Acts of Aggression).

1993b:5). By emphasizing external responses rather than causes within, and responsibilities of, the country of origin, the 1951 Convention favours an essentially reactive approach to refugee problems.

However, while a state is bound by the principle of *non-refoulement* and certain standards of treatment of refugees once they are on that state's territory, the 1951 Convention creates no direct obligation for states to admit asylum-seekers at the frontier or to grant asylum, whether interpreted as durable asylum or temporary refuge.[8] Thus, strictly speaking, there is no individualized right to be granted asylum in international law. However, some countries have a right of asylum written into their Constitutions. In Germany – the best-known example – parliament voted in May 1993 to amend its asylum laws so as to restrict access to its asylum systems in response to escalating numbers of applications. Since the 1951 Convention does not define 'persecution', nor does it define criteria by which to assess whether a fear of persecution may be 'well-founded', interpretation is left very much to the discretion of individual states.

The UNHCR Statute and 1951 Convention thus institutionalized elements of a more universalistic regime of refugee protection, but the instruments themselves reflected broad political interests of the Western states, and their application was left relatively open to political manipulation. Notwithstanding their obligation to respect the principle of *non-refoulement*, states were left more or less free to decide whether or not to admit refugees into their territory and whether or not to grant asylum, and they were left considerable room to determine for themselves what constitutes a 'well-founded fear of persecution'.

---

[8] Grahl-Madsen has argued that Article 33 only applies once the asylum-seeker has set foot in the country of refuge (Grahl-Madsen, 1972:223). However, the basic aim and purpose of the principle would seem to support a duty to allow entry if exclusion might result in *refoulement* (See Gunnel Stenberg, 1989:121–3). State practice is mixed in this respect.

Application of the 1951 Convention

During the 1950s and 1960s, the 1951 Convention proved both adequate for responding to the refugee problems faced by the Western states, and suited to their political interests. The majority of those seeking asylum in the West were people attempting to escape political repression and economic hardship in the Eastern bloc. Despite a reluctance to enter into any obligations over the granting of asylum, the Western states offered refuge to these groups in an almost automatic fashion ('presumptive refugee status'), even though the majority would not have been able to make a case for refugee status according to a strict interpretation of the 1951 Convention. By accepting exiles from the Eastern bloc as refugees, the Western countries could deal an ideological blow to the communist countries by stigmatizing them as persecutors, while simultaneously promoting Western liberal values.[9] Furthermore, owing to the imposition of exit restrictions by the Eastern bloc countries, the numbers were generally low. The refugees thus created no great burden for the receiving states, and the 1951 Convention could easily be applied on an individual case-by-case basis, as intended.[10] In the context of sudden exoduses, such as that from Hungary in 1956, case-by-case assessments were abandoned in favour of *prima facie* group determination.

Despite its suitability for application in the Western context, however, the 1951 Convention became more and more anachronistic as new refugee problems began emerging in other parts of the world. Its most serious shortcoming was overcome in 1967 with a Protocol which removed the temporal limitation,[11] and thus ex-

[9] In the USA, the refugee definition became tied to persons fleeing communism, until the passing of the Refugee Act of 1980. Note again, however, that the USA had not acceded to the 1951 Convention.

[10] The UNHCR Handbook on Procedures and Criteria for Determining Refugee Status advises that 'refugee status must normally be determined on an individual basis' and that 'an applicant for refugee status must normally show good reason why he individually fears persecution.' UNHCR, 1988:13.

[11] It removed the limitation to refugees who had become such as a result of events occurring before 1 January 1951. See the 1967 Protocol Relating to the Status of Refugees (United Nations, *Treaty Series*, vol. 606, p. 267). Text reproduced in the UNHCR Handbook (UNHCR, 1988: Annex III).

tended its field of application to mirror that of the UNHCR's Statute. However, by 1967, the activities of the UNHCR were already extending beyond assistance to refugees as defined in the Statute and the Convention.

The response to the exodus from Hungary in 1956 had set a precedent for more flexible approaches. Further *ad hoc* extensions of the UNHCR's mandate were secured under the so-called 'good offices' concept, according to which the UNHCR could respond to 'refugees who do not come within the competence of the United Nations'.[12] The UNHCR's 'good offices' were first invoked in the late 1950s and early 1960s to assist Chinese refugees in Hong Kong, Algerian refugees in Morocco and Tunisia, and Angolan refugees from Zaire. The UNHCR's more recent involvement in Iraq and the former Yugoslavia has been under its 'good offices'.

The introduction of the 'good offices' concept amounted to an open recognition that the UN refugee definition was not exhaustive. Indeed, the 1951 Convention and 1967 Protocol would have excluded most of those who have been forced to flee in the less developed world over the past three decades, and, in fact, most of those who were forced to move within Europe before 1951.[13] The majority would not have been able to demonstrate a personal 'well-founded fear of persecution', even though they were fleeing conditions – such as civil war, ethnic conflict, massive human rights abuses or famine – which had made their lives intolerably dangerous. Moreover, most refugees have fled in situations in which individual case-by-case assessments have been either impractical or impossible.

In 1969, the Organization for African Unity (OAU) adopted a Convention on Refugee Problems in Africa which encompassed a broader refugee concept. Article I of the Convention includes the UN definition, and then adds:

[12] General Assembly Resolution 1388 (XIV) of 20 November 1959.
[13] In this respect it is interesting to compare the expanded activities of the UNHCR with the earlier *ad hoc* and group-specific activities of the League of Nations.

The term 'refugee' shall also apply to every person who, owing to external aggression, occupation, foreign domination or events seriously disturbing public order in either part or the whole of his country of origin or nationality, is compelled to leave his place of habitual residence in order to seek refuge in another place outside his country of origin or nationality.

This definition facilitated flexible and pragmatic responses to a wide variety of refugee movements in Africa – responses which became increasingly important during the 1970s as more and more complex refugee problems began to emerge on the continent. In 1984, the Organization of American States (OAS) adopted the so-called 'Cartagena Declaration' which incorporated a similarly broad refugee definition.[14]

Very little change took place in the law and policy governing Western approaches to refugees, however. During the 1960s and 1970s, the West was hardly touched by the refugee crisis developing in Africa and other parts of the Third World. Consequently, there was little pressure for the West to reconsider its own policy regime. In respect of refugee movements in the 'South', the West adopted a 'donor's perspective' which was primarily concerned with the immediate needs of the refugees rather than causes and solutions, and according to which 'short-term operational considerations tended to strongly supplant any longer-term ones' (Coles, 1989:381–2).

However, by the 1980s, refugee problems of the less developed world had started to impinge directly on the West. This triggered the beginnings of a policy crisis in Western Europe which is now forcing a reassessment of the established policies of refugee protection.

---

[14] See *Annual Report of Inter-American Commission on Human Rights 1984–85*, OEA/Ser.L/II.66, doc. 10, rev. 1, at 190–93. See also Hathaway, 1991:19–21.

The emergence of a policy crisis in Western Europe

The Indochinese refugee crisis was one of the first refugee problems of the less developed world in which the West became directly involved. The West's involvement in the crisis stemmed from an overarching sense of responsibility to act when the Southeast Asian receiving states began turning the refugees away. Because return to Vietnam could not be contemplated by the West, and because the 'first asylum' countries could not be persuaded to accept the refugees for permanent settlement, the only apparent 'solution' was resettlement, primarily in the West. The process of resettlement heralded a new era of 'South–North' refugee movements. This stimulated little anxiety at the time due to the fact that the West's involvement was voluntary, and the refugees' movement controlled. As Martin observes, the new efforts still fitted 'rather readily within established assumptions and patterns, and gave little cause for Western publics to think that refugee programs greatly threatened the sovereign's usual prerogative to exercise deliberate control over immigration' (Martin, 1988:4).

By the 1980s, however, this situation was changing as increasing numbers of asylum-seekers began fleeing independently to the West from their countries and regions of origin. 'Spontaneous' (as opposed to managed) arrivals of asylum-seekers had, in fact, been rising steadily since the early 1970s, but it was not until the mid-1980s that numbers began escalating substantially. According to UNHCR data, the numbers arriving in the European Community increased from under 70,000 in 1983 to over 200,000 in 1989.[15] The reasons for this increase are not entirely clear. Improved air transport communications are often cited,[16] although it may be that the well-publicized resettlement programmes of the 1970s were as significant, opening up as they did a new prospect of finding asylum in the West (Coles, 1992:34–5; and Martin, 1988:5). Also significant was the worldwide increase in the global refugee

[15] UNHCR Regional Office for the European Institutions, Brussels, January 1993. Note that since the collapse of the Eastern bloc, arrivals have escalated even more sharply: from over 300,000 in 1990 to over 500,000 in 1992.
[16] See, for example, Loescher, 1992b:10.

populations, which increased from approximately 10 million to 17 million between 1985 and 1991, excluding those displaced within their own countries. Set against these figures, the numbers of asylum-seekers arriving in Western Europe appear very modest. However, their impact on refugee policy and on the political climate in which refugee problems are approached in Europe has been enormous. The fact that the arrival of these new asylum-seekers has been unregulated has been an obvious cause for concern to states which are already nervous over the issue of immigration. Yet the new arrivals have also raised questions of a more fundamental nature relating to the efficacy of the policies in place. As their numbers have increased, the limitations of existing policy have become proportionately more visible.

First, the numbers involved, especially in recent years, and the unwillingness of states to resort to presumptive or *prima facie* determinations, have placed immense pressures on asylum systems in both administrative and financial terms.[17] The financial cost associated with the support of asylum-seekers and the case-by-case adjudication procedures followed in Western Europe are estimated to run into billions of dollars per year (Widgren, 1991). Because the majority of asylum-seekers have eventually been given leave to remain, or have remained despite the refusal of asylum, this system appears in practice to have degenerated into little more than an extremely expensive and cumbersome system of status determination.

Substantive problems such as these go only part of the way towards explaining the current policy crisis, however. Just as significant is the fact that the real or perceived costs associated with refugee protection – whether they be economic, political or social – are no longer offset by either a powerful political imperative or an overriding humanitarian concern.

[17] These pressures have been greatest in Germany, which, since 1989, has received over half of the total number of asylum-seekers arriving in Western Europe. The member states of the European Community together received an estimated 558,600 asylum-seekers in 1992, roughly double the number in 1990. UNHCR Regional Office for the European Institutions, Brussels, January 1993.

Why the political balance no longer applies is explained by the end of the Cold War, and the fact that to offer refuge to the new asylum-seekers, whether from inside or outside Europe, no longer serves any obvious strategic or political interest. Thus the moral, legal and humanitarian bases of refugee policy in Western Europe – particularly its emphasis on asylum – are only now really being put to the test for the first time. Asylum-seekers have become a 'burden', and assistance to them is now seen as much in terms of generosity or charity as in terms of moral or legal obligation (Singer and Singer, 1988). At a time of economic recession and political insecurity, this generosity is likely to be less forthcoming. Thus, an external political interest which favoured the granting of asylum has given way to internal political pressures which work to restrict it.

Why the humanitarian underpinning of asylum policy has weakened may be partly explained in terms of 'compassion fatigue'. However, more important is a shift which has taken place in the way asylum-seekers are perceived. As Martin reports, the 'spontaneous' arrivals of the 1980s and 1990s have upset a balance based on a perception of relative danger or hardship which has implicitly supported the assistance accorded to refugees in poorer parts of the world. When asylum-seekers flee their country of origin for an uncertain future in equally poor and sometimes equally unstable countries, their willingness to endure harsh conditions in situations of exile has been taken as testimony to their desperate plight and need for assistance. Yet when they arrive in the West, an element of suspicion may creep in as to their 'real' motives for flight. As Martin observes:

These suspicions are probably exaggerated when they take the form of assumptions that the new asylum seekers had *no* good reason for leaving home. But they may take a more accurate form: that an important percentage of those who now move directly are people who would not have chosen to leave home ... if they thought they were moving to a camp in Honduras or the Sudan rather than the greater benefits available in most Western countries. The motives of *these* new asylum seekers, whatever their deeper merit, do not carry the same connotations of specialness that built and sustains the unique provision for refugees, at least in the eyes of much of the public in Western nations. (Martin, 1988:10–11)

At a time when the media is full of images of refugees and other populations in desperate need of assistance in Africa, former Yugoslavia and other parts of the world, the importance of these concerns should not be underestimated. Fundamental questions arise relating to the West's overall responsibilities to the world's millions of refugees and displaced persons. The financial cost of assisting the minority of asylum-seekers who manage to reach Western Europe now amounts to several times the total budget of the UNHCR – a budget which is intended to stretch to refugee assistance worldwide. There is no obvious way out of this dilemma which would avoid doing serious damage to the principle of asylum in Western Europe.

In political terms, this problem is made more complicated by the fact that, irrespective of their needs, many asylum-seekers do not fit the 1951 refugee definition. Since the mid-1970s, the Council of Europe has been pressing for a regional instrument to establish a codified system of protection for refugees not covered by the 1951 Convention, but its efforts have not been successful.[18] Consequently, while the majority of so-called 'de facto' refugees have been accorded some form of temporary refuge, they have only been considered on a discretionary basis by individual states. Because their needs are less well-defined, and because protection in such cases is not granted on the basis of an international legal instrument, the systems under which protection is offered easily appear muddled, at least to the general public. Moreover, because those who are offered refuge but fail to meet the 1951 criteria are not granted refugee status, their position is not accorded the same 'moral worth' as that accorded to victims of persecution (Zolberg

---

[18] See, for example, Council of Europe Recommendation 773 (1976) and Recommendation R (84) 1 (1984). Note that the UNHCR has also been pressing for such an instrument.

et al., 1989:269). Indeed, as discussed below, it is now not uncommon for politicians in Western Europe to exploit the difficulties in applying the Convention by labelling all those who fail to meet its terms as 'bogus' refugees or 'mere' economic migrants.

In this context, it is important to note that the 1951 Convention is being interpreted in progressively restrictive terms in Western Europe, with the effect that many of those who might have been granted refugee status five or ten years ago will now be granted some other 'humanitarian' protective status. Indeed, human rights advocates have argued that 'de facto' refugee status or refugee 'B'-status is increasingly resorted to as a way of side-stepping the obligations which attach to the granting of refugee status.

Also important, however, is the fact that, since 1989, asylum systems have come under increasing strain from applicants – particularly from Eastern/Central Europe or the former Soviet Union – who use asylum systems as a means of entering Western Europe for reasons other than that of seeking protection. This is a problem which not only governments, but also human rights pressure groups have found difficult to deal with. Many of the latter feel that to acknowledge the problem openly will play into the hands of governments which are now keen to rally support for restrictive measures with more general effect. And, while governments may indeed be prone to exaggerating the problem of 'abusive' applications in order to support restrictive measures, nevertheless they do have a problem that is not at all easy to reconcile with an overall commitment to the principle of asylum.

The sustainability of a policy regime which places all the emphasis on asylum when states are increasingly reluctant to grant it, which relies on a refugee definition that excludes most of the refugees with which it is having to cope, and which – largely because of the West's concern to maintain its strict application – encourages extremely expensive and cumbersome case-by-case determinations irrespective of the numbers involved, is becoming increasingly uncertain. The limits of the regime's utility outside the confines of Cold War politics were revealed over three decades ago when complex refugee problems began to emerge in other parts of the world. The limits of its utility in the European context began to show when Europe itself began to be touched by these problems. Now, as Europe is faced with new complex refugee crises of its own, the tensions are more manifest than ever.

Towards a new comprehensive regime?
Unless Western Europe can look beyond immediate political concerns and adapt its refugee policies to reflect and cope with the complex realities of the refugee phenomenon, even asylum for victims of persecution – a 'vital, albeit discrete, aspect of refugee protection' – may be threatened (UNHCR, 1992b:5). As stated recently by the UN High Commissioner for Refugees, 'the growing scale and complexity of the refugee problem, as well as the changed international context, make clear the inadequacy of asylum as the whole response' (Ogata, 1992:3). The end of the Cold War has brought both positive and negative prospects for the development of refugee policy in Western Europe.

On the positive side, the removal of the Cold War political imperative, a broadened security agenda, and a new international emphasis on human and minority rights and conflict prevention and resolution have facilitated more open consideration of the complex political roots of refugee movements, and of the complex nature of the movements themselves. In this context, more consideration is being given to how 'solutions' to refugee movements can be related more closely to the causes, and thus to conditions in countries of origin. And, at the same time as attention is shifting to causes and solutions in the refugee field, so the United Nations is showing a greater – albeit uncertain – willingness to examine internal situations and civil wars as threats to international peace and security, and to see the internal protection of human rights as a matter of concern to the international community. Refugee flows are no longer seen in isolation from the broader issues of peace and security and human rights in the country or region of origin. In Europe, a new urgency is forcing the pace.

This new political climate is reflected in a shift of emphasis within the UNHCR. Its strategy has been summarized by the High Commissioner as having three core objectives: 'prevention, preparedness and solutions'. Consideration has shifted towards protecting people's 'right to stay', as opposed to people's right to flee. As stated by the High Commissioner, the new strategy 'complements asylum outside the country of origin with prevention and solution-oriented activities *inside* the country of origin' (Ogata, 1993a:3).

A 'Note on International Protection' submitted by the present High Commissioner to the UNHCR Executive Committee in October 1992 includes under the heading of 'indirect prevention': support for the 'peacemaking and peace-keeping activities of the United Nations Secretary-General', and 'preventive measures in the areas of human rights promotion'. Under the heading of 'direct prevention', the Note includes 'the undertaking of specific activities inside countries of origin so that people do not feel compelled to leave to cross borders in search of protection', such as 'international monitoring of basic human rights and the physical safety of internally displaced persons'. In terms of 'solutions', the emphasis is placed on repatriation – a process which depends on the resolution of the (political) problems which gave rise to refugee movement, and in which 'the protection needs of refugees [must be balanced] against the political imperative towards resolving refugee problems' (UNHCR, 1992a).

UNHCR activity has thus moved clearly into the realms of 'comprehensive response' in which its non-political mandate is increasingly difficult to uphold. As noted by the High Commissioner, 'as the focus of ... activities shifts gradually from relatively stable conditions in the country of asylum to the more turbulent and often evolutionary process in the country of origin, it becomes linked to the political efforts of the United Nations to bring about peace and security' (Ogata, 1993a:3). Kathleen Newland observes the direct tensions which this shift has brought about in the context of Bosnia–Herzegovina, where the UNHCR has been trying to reach an extremely difficult balance between the purely humanitarian concern to relieve suffering and the more political concern not to facilitate displacement by evacuating target populations from zones of conflict (Newland, 1993a:98).

Reservations connected with the emerging regime
As the UNHCR has begun involving itself in more comprehensive efforts, it has begun cooperating with more or less innovatory approaches to refugee protection which emphasize the prevention of flight and the return of those who have fled, including the creation of 'safe areas' for vulnerable populations within their country of origin (Iraq and the former Yugoslavia); and the expansion and consolidation of the concept of 'temporary protection' outside the country of origin.

Looked at from the standpoint that asylum is increasingly difficult to rely upon as a durable 'solution' (particularly in situations of large-scale movement), and from the standpoint that exile is itself a human rights problem which should be avoided or resolved wherever possible (Coles, 1992:35), these initiatives appear essentially positive. However, a number of important questions arise when one considers their actual or potential implementation on the ground.

The concept of 'safe areas' begs the obvious questions of what constitutes 'safe' and how that safety is to be assured or maintained. Moves to establish safe areas in Bosnia–Herzegovina have already run into problems owing to the extreme volatility of the situation there; and in Iraq, where safe areas were operationally easier to establish, it is not at all clear how much longer, and on what basis, they will continue to be protected. Similarly, the concept of 'temporary protection' begs the obvious question: how temporary? And it raises the important question of what standards should apply to the concept of 'protection' (as compared, for example, with the protection standards applied to refugee status under the 1951 Convention).

Indeed, the success of any response in which the stress is placed on flight-prevention and return is entirely contingent upon a range

of often highly unpredictable political factors, including developments in the country of origin (e.g. those which determine whether
return, or the establishment or dismantling of safe areas, is possible), and upon the capacity and will of the international community
to act. Both are factors which will vary considerably from one
situation to the next. There is as yet no clear codification of the new
strategies, and no clear institutional structure within which they
can be pursued. The UNHCR can only pursue preventive or
protective activities within a country of origin under its 'good
offices', and only then when requested to do so by the UN
Secretary-General and/or Security Council (as in Iraq and the
former Yugoslavia); and, while the UN has moved towards support for humanitarian intervention, it is not at all clear that its
activities to date have set a precedent for future action. Moreover,
as indicated by current developments in the former Yugoslavia, the
difficulty of the situations in which the UN is likely to become
embroiled means that prospects of success will be highly uncertain.

Given the complexity of most population displacements, there
is a strong argument for maintaining an essentially flexible approach to current and potential refugee flows. Thus, for example,
population displacements which develop suddenly will require
different responses from those which take place gradually. Flows
generated as a consequence of a deliberate political or military
strategy – such as in the former Yugoslavia – will create different
political problems from those resulting from more generalized
inter-communal tensions and conflict, such as in Somalia. And
those which take place in situations where receiving states are
relatively open to protecting refugees – such as in Armenia and
Azerbaijan – raise different questions from those where receiving
states are more hostile, as was the case when Turkey closed its
borders to Kurds fleeing Iraq after the Gulf war.[19] Yet, without any
basic framework for action, there is a danger that preventive and
protective activities will depend increasingly on differential politi-

[19] See Newland, 1993b.

cal and economic interest, as was the case in Europe during the first half of this century.[20]

A great deal of attention has been paid recently to the institutional problems besetting multilateral responses to refugee movements and other humanitarian crises. One result has been the establishment of a UN Department of Humanitarian Affairs and the appointment of a UN Emergency Relief Coordinator. Although the complexity of the issues does call for a better coordination and division of labour between the various institutions involved, it could be argued that the central problem today is not the adequacy of international institutions, but the political will to use or support them (Coles, 1992:39).[21] Whether there is the political will to establish a stronger protective regime outside the scope of the 1951 Convention, and to support intergovernmental and nongovernmental institutions to their best capacity in this context is possibly the most salient question to be asked.

The question of political will is crucial, for it is possible to look at recent initiatives not in terms of the emergence of a more positive policy stance, but rather as symptoms of states' persisting, or even increasing, reluctance to extend their obligations in respect of displaced populations. Looked at from this standpoint, the uncertain concepts of 'safe areas' and 'temporary protection' can be seen as primarily indicative of a general weakening of support for the principle of asylum, and thus as representative of an expanding political 'no man's land' in respect of refugee protection: where refugees' safe return is difficult to achieve, where the 'frontline' receiving states lack the will or resources to offer them durable protection, and where potential 'second' asylum countries, such as

[20] Note that a Resolution on 'Certain Common Guidelines as Regards the Admission of Particularly Vulnerable Groups of Persons from the Former Yugoslavia' issued by the EC Ministers Responsible for Immigration at Copenhagen in June 1993 is reminiscent of the group-specific (and thus variable) responses of the League of Nations during the interwar period. See Ad Hoc Group on Immigration, 1993.

[21] Note, in this context, the problems the UNHCR has recently had in securing financial support for its humanitarian efforts in the former Yugoslavia. See *The Guardian*, 12 July 1993.

those of Western Europe, resist pressure for their resettlement.

In the short term, the real test may be whether governments have the political will to support and maintain their asylum policies in the absence of any clear alternatives. The world's population of (both internally and externally) displaced persons is estimated to exceed 30 million. This is primarily a tragedy for the poorer and less stable parts of the world in which these populations are (and will continue to be) concentrated.[22] However, it is also a tragedy from which the countries of Western Europe cannot be isolated. Whatever success is achieved in terms of prevention, people will continue to be forced to move – many of them across borders, many of them into Western Europe, and many of them with little prospect of safe return to their country or region of origin.

Current developments in asylum policy

The problems now facing Western Europe's asylum policies are clearly serious, and substantial adaptations may be needed if asylum is to survive as a central pillar of refugee protection.

Some positive developments can be discerned in this respect. First, efforts to harmonize or coordinate the asylum policies of the EC member states have created a new pressure for more uniform application of the 1951 Convention and 1967 Protocol and more uniform standards of treatment for asylum-seekers, including the possibility of a clearer codification of protection standards for refugees who do not come within the United Nations definition. A Centre for Information, Discussion and Exchange on Asylum (CIREA) has been set up within the EC Council of Ministers, which, *inter alia*, will keep countries better informed of one another's policies and standards, and which should promote more informed and more consensual appraisal of the situations in countries of origin.[23]

[22] See US Committee for Refugees, 1993.
[23] Note, however, a Resolution on European immigration policy adopted by the European Parliament on 15 July 1993, which criticizes CIREA since its operations 'are not based on an independent statute and are not sufficiently accessible'.

Second, the European Community's so-called 'Dublin Convention' determining the state responsible for examining asylum applications,[24] attempts to resolve the problem of 'refugees in orbit' (i.e. refugees for whom no state is willing to take responsibility), and thereby introduces for the first time a positive responsibility for states to examine asylum requests. Article 3 states that 'Member States undertake to examine the application of any alien who applies at the border or in their territory to any one of them for asylum.'[25] Moreover, the Declaration on Principles Governing External Aspects of Migration Policy issued by the EC Council of Ministers at Edinburgh in December 1992 includes a statement that, in the context of flight from the former Yugoslavia, states 'reaffirm their belief that the burden of financing relief activities should be shared more equitably by the international community' (European Council, 1992), although the translation of rhetoric into practice in this respect has so far been limited. Finally, most states have started to reorganize their administrative arrangements for dealing with asylum applications in an attempt to reduce backlogs and delays and to reduce the bureaucratic 'weight' (and therefore costs) of their present adjudication structures.

However, other developments indicate that greater priority is being given to more defensive policies and procedures which will have – or are intended to have – a direct effect in deterring or restricting asylum applications in Western Europe. It is, for exam-

[24] The Convention Determining the State Responsible for Examining Applications for Asylum Lodged in One of the Member States of the European Communities, signed by the Ministers Responsible for Immigration at their meeting in Dublin on 15 June 1990. The text of the Convention is reproduced in the Bulletin of the European Communities 6–1990.
[25] However, because the Dublin Convention places responsibility for examining applications on the 'first host country' within the EC area, it is likely to encourage states to harmonize up to the most restrictive policies and procedures. Moreover, as Amnesty International has argued, prior to full harmonization, an asylum-seeker may be compelled to lodge an application for asylum in a country whose procedures lack certain safeguards. See Amnesty International, 1991:25. This is also a concern connected with the concept of 'third host country' (referring to first host countries outside the European Community), as discussed below.

ple, now common practice for West European states to impose visa restrictions on countries generating refugees. This practice is supported by the Treaty on European Union, which, under Article 100c, states that 'in the event of an emergency situation in a third country posing a threat of a sudden inflow of nationals from that country into the Community, the Council may ... *introduce*' – rather than remove – 'a visa requirement for nationals from the country in question' (emphasis added). It is worth noting, for example, that the majority of EC member states now require visas for nationals of Bosnia–Herzegovina.[26] Visa requirements are given greater effect by their frequent combination with carrier sanctions, a policy according to which airlines and other carriers are fined for bringing into a country any person who lacks the requisite documentation for entry.[27] Carrier sanctions are included as a provision of the Schengen Implementing Convention, and are almost certainly included in the External Borders Convention.[28]

Such measures are allowed according to the letter of the 1951 Convention and 1967 Protocol, for these instruments only impose an obligation on states not to send back refugees to a country where they might suffer persecution once they have arrived in the state in question. However, they clearly conflict with the spirit of these instruments in so far as they constitute direct obstacles to flight from such countries, and fall indiscriminately on all categories of asylum-seeker, including the most deserving cases. As such, they represent a direct challenge to the principle of asylum.

More recent developments under the rubric of cooperation and harmonization among the EC member states reflect an agenda which stresses negative before positive responsibilities *vis-à-vis*

[26] At 30 April 1993, only Denmark, Italy, Spain and Portugal and France did not require visas for nationals of Bosnia–Herzegovina. France requires a letter of sponsorship. See UNHCR, 1993.
[27] For a discussion of the effects of carrier sanctions on asylum systems, see Danish Refugee Council and Danish Center of Human Rights, 1991.
[28] Note that the draft External Borders Convention is still officially confidential. A draft was circulated by the European Parliament's Committee on Civil Liberties and Internal Affairs in early 1992. This draft includes provisions for the introduction of carrier sanctions.

asylum-seekers. Thus, at the London meeting of the Ad Hoc Group on Immigration in November/December 1992, EC Ministers agreed to Resolutions on 'manifestly unfounded applications for asylum' and 'host third countries', and to a Conclusion on the concept of countries 'in which there is generally no serious risk of persecution' (the 'safe country' principle) (Ad Hoc Group on Immigration, 1992). These are not legal agreements, but they carry considerable political weight, and the assumption is that their provisions will be incorporated into national legislation.[29]

According to the notion of 'manifestly unfounded applications', states will separate from normal procedures those claims which are deemed fraudulent or which are found to have been lodged in 'bad faith', and deal with them in an accelerated procedure. This is an important measure designed to relieve asylum systems of the pressures imposed by 'abusive' applications. However, as Amnesty International has pointed out, the Resolution reached within the framework of the Ad Hoc Group raises serious concerns regarding procedural standards for the treatment of asylum claims, including access to legal advice and appeal procedures. Moreover, the Resolution broadens the definition of such applications beyond that put forward by the UNHCR,[30] to include a number of criteria of which some appear, in the words of Amnesty International, 'dangerously vague and far-reaching' (Amnesty International, 1992:10). Amnesty has argued that although measures to speed the process of examining asylum requests should be welcomed,

[29] Note that Germany's amended asylum law, which took effect on 1 July 1993, incorporates all three concepts. The United Kingdom's Asylum and Immigration Appeals Act, which also came into effect on 1 July 1993, includes the notion of claims 'without foundation'; and new Immigration Rules on Asylum include the concept of 'third host country' (HMSO House of Commons Paper No.725, published on 5 July 1993).

[30] The UNHCR Executive Committee defines the applications in question as 'clearly fraudulent or not related to the criteria for granting refugee status laid down in the 1951 ... Convention ... nor to any other criteria justifying the granting of asylum'. See Conclusion No.30 (XXXIV) of the 34th Session of the UNHCR Executive Committee (1983).

the proposed reforms to accelerate procedures and to identify which claims should be defined as 'manifestly unfounded' do not sufficiently respect international standards
for the protection of refugees. Serious deficiencies still exist
in policy and practice in the member states, and current
proposals to harmonize the application of these policies will
only exacerbate the risk that those in need of protection will
be returned and put at risk of further persecution (Amnesty
International, 1992:2).

The Resolution on 'host third countries' refers to asylum claims
in cases where the asylum-seeker has passed through, or spent time
in, another country where s/he could have been expected to seek
protection. It holds that if there is a third host country, 'the
application for refugee status may not be examined and the asylum
applicant may be sent to that country'. Although the Resolution
contains an explicit recognition of the responsibility of states to
make an enquiry into the conditions in the third host country before
returning an asylum-seeker there,[31] the Resolution contains no
reference to procedural and legal standards to be applied in the
case of such returns. Indeed, in setting out criteria establishing
whether a country may be considered a third host country, the
Resolution makes no reference to whether that country should be
signatory to the 1951 Convention and 1967 Protocol, nor does it set
out any criteria regarding standards of treatment. It simply states
that the asylum-seeker, if sent back to such a country, 'should not
be exposed to torture or inhuman or degrading treatment', and
that the applicant 'must be afforded effective protection ... against
refoulement'. As noted by Amnesty International, the Resolution
is insufficient in that it does not stipulate that protection in the third
host country must be both effective and durable. It is thus quite
possible that refugee flows will be deflected back to countries of
transit, such as those in Eastern/Central Europe, where asylum

[31] Note that the absence of such a requirement from the Dublin Convention
has been a cause for concern among human rights and other pressure groups.
See Amnesty International, 1992.

systems cannot yet guarantee reliable protection in the sense of the 1951 Convention and 1967 Protocol.

Like the readmission agreements (discussed in Chapter 3), the application of the 'third host country' concept in asylum policy represents a direct attempt to create a protective 'buffer zone' around Western Europe. Such measures call into question the prospects of refugee policies being developed which go 'beyond national interests or short-term political considerations' (Ogata, 1992:3), and which are based, among other things, on solidarity and 'burden-sharing'. In fact the readmission agreements do set out a framework for burden-sharing, but this is limited largely to financial assistance, and thus represents only a very restricted interpretation of the concept. As noted in Chapter 3, one of the major concerns of the Visegrad states is now immigration rather than emigration, including potential flows of asylum-seekers back into their countries from Western Europe.

The Conclusion on 'safe countries' is equally defensive, the aim being to deal with applicants from such countries in accelerated procedures, such as those introduced to deal with claims which are found to be 'manifestly unfounded'. The introduction of the 'safe country' concept seems sensible in principle, given the pressures caused by large numbers of applicants from countries in which the risk of persecution would seem relatively low. Indeed, it is a concept which is already widely applied in Western Europe, if only informally and only for the purposes of deciding the validity of individual claims. Again, however, a number of concerns have been raised by human rights advocates and by the UNHCR. Some of the concerns mirror those raised in connection with the notion of 'manifestly unfounded' claims. Two further reservations deserve particular mention, however. First, there is the question of the criteria according to which a country may be labelled 'safe'. In particular, there is a danger of foreign policy and other considerations (e.g. the number of asylum-seekers from a particular country) creeping into the categorization. And, second, there is the fact that the 'safe country' concept constitutes a *de facto* geographical reservation to the 1951 Convention[32] if it is formalized in such a way that applicants from certain countries are excluded from normal asylum procedures and denied any possibility of being granted refugee status.

It is thus questionable whether current developments in asylum policy reflect 'courage, vision and political will', as recently called for by the United Nations High Commissioner for Refugees (Ogata, 1992:3). Instead, it seems that national interests and short-term political considerations prevail. As with immigration, the treatment of the asylum issue has suffered from the reactive and defensive political climate which has followed the collapse of the Eastern bloc. And as with immigration, this has resulted in an increasing preoccupation with restriction and control.

Asylum: an immigration or a human rights issue?
The current concern with restricting access to asylum systems in Western Europe indicates that asylum is increasingly treated as an immigration rather than a human rights issue there. From a purely functional point of view, this may not be seen as particularly objectionable – both immigration and asylum policies involve the entry and residence of foreign nationals, and thus it may seem quite practical to link the two issues together. Moreover, they do overlap to some extent. As noted above, it has never been easy to posit a clearly applicable distinction between 'refugees' and 'migrants'; and asylum systems have undoubtedly fallen prey to a certain amount of 'abuse' from applicants trying to use asylum as a means of gaining entry to the West.

However, as Philip Rudge observes, 'where the refugee issue collapses into other issues, ... the human rights dimension is lost sight of ... It is extraordinary but true that even in the last decade of the twentieth century it is still necessary to restate the obvious: that at its root and in its evolution the refugee question is funda-

[32] Prohibited by Article 42, and probably contrary to Article 3 of the 1951 Convention.

mentally a human rights issue' (Rudge, 1992:102). The fact that the recent amendment of Germany's asylum laws[33] was reported in the British media as a restriction of the country's previous 'open door immigration policy'[34] reflects the degree to which the two issues have become confused in the public mind.

This confusion may be seen to serve a political purpose for governments concerned to restrict asylum inflows. The public may put pressure on governments to control or restrict the numbers of asylum-seekers entering a country, but it is also highly sensitive to any action which may be seen to cause human suffering. Indeed, as Martin notes, governments are frequently caught in a political crossfire between 'alarmed restrictionists' and 'vocal refugee advocates' (Martin, 1988:13). By positing asylum in terms of immigration, governments implicitly play down the humanitarian aspect of the refugee problem, and may thereby defuse the public's sensitivity to the potential humanitarian consequences of any restrictive measures introduced.

Although, overall, this may not be a self-conscious strategy, some politicians and policy-makers have exaggerated the asylum–immigration link to create the impression that only a small minority of asylum-seekers (i.e. those who fit a very restrictive interpretation of the 1951 Convention) are in 'genuine' need of protection. In so doing, they play on the fears and anxieties which surround the immigration issue, and thereby strengthen the hand of the restrictionist camp. Indeed, the term 'asylum-seeker' has become progressively divorced from that of 'refugee' in recent years, the latter now more commonly used to describe displaced populations within the former Yugoslavia or other areas of the world where the public is fully aware of the extreme suffering, and where the need for assistance is obvious.

A debate carried out in such terms fails to capture what is singular about the asylum dilemma, nor does it reflect the full complexities of the problem. It cannot, therefore, form a basis for

[33] See, for example, *The Times*, 2 July 1993; *International Herald Tribune*, 2 July 1993; *The Daily Telegraph*, 1 July 1993.
[34] BBC Radio 4's 'Today' programme, 26 May 1993.

informed public debate, or for a rational refugee policy. Moreover, while it may in the short term help to create a political 'breathing-space' for restrictive policies to be introduced, in the longer term it may be a dangerous political path to tread, for if Western Europe is to continue to offer asylum to those who most need it, the support and compassion of the public will be of critical importance.

Asylum certainly has its limitations as a response to modern-day refugee problems, and it is therefore imperative that preventative policies are pursued wherever possible in existing and potential situations of population displacement. However, these alternative strategies still have a long way to go before they can be relied upon. In the meantime, asylum will continue to represent an integral component of the international refugee 'regime' if refugee protection is to survive as a central principle and basis for policy. As argued in Chapter 5, Western Europe's asylum systems will need to be supported on this basis.

5

Towards an active policy regime

International migration is a discrete phenomenon only in the sense that it involves the movement of persons across state borders. When one looks beyond this definition, it is clear that one is not dealing with a single issue. Migration represents only one component of much broader processes of political, economic, social and cultural change, and varies as much as the processes which give rise to and result from it. The diversity of issues touched on by the phenomenon is thus considerable. Immigrant integration, for example, raises fundamental questions relating to national identity and the structure of society. Control of 'economic' immigration provokes debate about the interaction of economic structures and the movement of persons, and about the limits of state control. Finally, the asylum issue bears on the responsibility of states in the context of human rights.

This complexity, coupled with the political sensitivity of many of the issues involved, has meant that West European governments have failed to develop policies suitable for managing migration in a comprehensive fashion. Instead, policies have emerged as a series of 'knee-jerk' reactions to problems as they arise, and have generally taken the form of direct enforcement mechanisms, as opposed to strategies designed to manage the broader causes and consequences.

Since the end of the Cold War, the effectiveness of these mechanisms has come under unprecedented scrutiny as greater attention has focused on the intensification of migration pressures around the region's periphery – both new or potential pressures in Central/Eastern Europe and the former Soviet Union, and more long-standing pressures in the 'South'. The large-scale exodus from Albania, the outbreak of war in the former Yugoslavia, and the substantial escalation in arrivals of asylum-seekers (particularly into Germany) have all contributed to a new perception that there is a threat from migration, and to a rapid erosion of confidence in the adequacy of the policies in place.

The governments of Western Europe are now clearly in a difficult position over immigration. It is increasingly apparent that immigration cannot be regulated entirely on the basis of direct controls (see Chapter 3). However, there are no obvious alternatives which are likely to have an immediate and visible impact. 'Immediate' and 'visible' are the operative words, for governments are now more sensitive than ever to widespread public anxiety over immigration, and policy-makers are determined to be seen to be doing something to control it. They cannot afford to pursue policies which are substantially out of line with majority public opinion, for to do so might entail the risk of a political backlash which could further restrict their room for manoeuvre. The result is an extremely reactive posture, and a degree of confusion which frustrates the development of the kind of active policies needed to meet current challenges.

How policy-makers are to escape from this situation is by no means obvious. As discussed in Chapter 3, the persistence of unregulated immigration is impelling governments to place greater emphasis on enforcement measures. Yet the longer this process continues, the longer it will be before more active policies can be introduced, and a greater degree of order brought about. A more forward-looking policy regime is likely to rest on more positive migration policies, yet these would be difficult to introduce in the present political climate.

In the light of these observations, it may be best to consider how a more constructive policy debate might be fostered before discussing possible substantive changes to existing policy.

The short term: fostering a constructive policy debate

It would be a mistake to overlook the importance of the prevailing political culture in shaping migration policies and the debates which surround them.[1] Although different countries in Western Europe have exhibited important variations in orientation towards immigration and related issues (Collinson, 1993), in all, public opinion has manifested a political or cultural resistance to immigration; and this, in turn, encourages a negative or defensive policy stance, as Chapter 3 has shown. Yet it would also be a mistake to assume that public opinion is entirely static and inflexible. Public perceptions of the immigration issue may be influenced considerably by politicians and policy-makers, or by the media. Indeed, it is possible that policy-makers have wittingly or unwittingly reinforced the public anxieties to which they must be seen to be responding, through continual references to the migration 'problem' or the migration 'threat'. As argued in a recent Council of Europe report:

> official attitudes are of crucial importance. The role of the State authorities as leaders of opinion, especially in delicate matters concerning immigration, is often underestimated. The messages of government authorities reach a very wide public, including those working in public services who take their cue from the attitudes expressed, explicitly or implicitly, by political leaders (Council of Europe, 1991:25).

How, then, might policy-makers shift the debate in a more positive direction, and reach beyond a policy regime predicated entirely on defensive concepts of restriction and control, while remaining responsive to public concerns? A number of measures would appear feasible in this context.

Openness

First, more open and transparent policy-making is desirable. At the level of the European Community, the current practice is to carry

---

[1] See, for example, Livi-Bacci, 1991.

out important intergovernmental discussions on migration policy behind closed doors.[2] In 1991, the EC Ministers responsible for immigration acknowledged 'criticism [which] is particularly aimed at the fact that deliberations are not public' and advised that consideration be given 'to the manner in which contacts with external organisations could be formed in the framework of discussions on a uniform European immigration policy and how the results could be presented'. Indeed, they went on to state that it is:

> impossible to over-rate the importance which political circles must attach to the question of immigration policy in a period of great tension; the more the activities undertaken in the harmonization process are favourably perceived by society and the political world, the greater will be the chances of success (Ad Hoc Group on Immigration, 1991:17).

And yet the climate is still one dominated by secrecy, and the policy-making process at the European level is still opaque. Precisely because the subject is such a sensitive one, the closed approach adds to the general climate of anxiety, and reinforces the suspicions of those uneasy about restrictive policies. This contributes to a further polarization and politicization of the debate in a way that works against the development of rational policy.

Sharpening categories
Second, it might be helpful to begin deconstructing the migration 'problem' by sharpening the categories in discourse on the issue. Only on the basis of an explicit recognition of the different types of migration, the various contexts in which it takes place, the different reasons for it, and consequences that follow, will it be possible to move beyond a reactive environment in which all immigration is seen as a problem, and one to be prevented. There has, until now, been an obfuscation of the migration issue: those types of migration

[2] Note that this is facilitated by the fact that governments have not recognized Community competence in migration policy (as noted in Chapter 3). Discussions among the Schengen states are carried out in a similarly secretive fashion.

which arouse particular anxiety – particularly unauthorized immigration and 'abusive' asylum claims – have become synonymous with migration in general; and problems largely specific to particular countries are seen as common to all the countries of Western Europe. Many state-specific problems, such as undocumented immigration into the Southern European states, are likely to remain so despite the abolition of border controls within Schengen/the European Community/the European Economic Area, as migration trends are strongly influenced by region- or country-specific economic, political and social conditions which will continue to vary from one state to another. In 1992 the UK received little more than 20,000 applications for asylum, whereas Germany received over 500,000. According to the International Passenger Survey, overall net immigration into the UK in 1991 was an estimated 28,000 (267,000 people entered the UK, but this was balanced by an estimated 239,000 who left); net immigration into Germany in the same year has been estimated by the Rheinisch-Westfälisches Institut für Wirtschaftsforschung to have exceeded 150,000 (Office of Population Censuses and Surveys, 1993:ix; and Gieseck et al., 1993).

A starting-point for a clearer articulation of policy is provided by the fact that distinctions between different categories of immigration are already made by existing policy. Indeed, almost all the states of Western Europe allow continuous and regular immigration for certain categories. These include family immigration, temporary education-related immigration, and certain categories of worker migration, such as professional, managerial and technical (PMT) worker immigration, temporary training-related immigration, and some unskilled seasonal or frontier migration. All countries are still partially open to asylum inflows; and countries still periodically pursue what might be termed 'national-specific' flows, such as the migration of ethnic Germans to Germany from Central/Eastern Europe and the former Soviet Union. If this immigration is to continue, toleration of, and trust in, the policies under which it takes place will be more easily maintained if the reasons and basis for it are clearly understood by the general public

92

(Spencer, 1993). Such an understanding could relate not to a failure to implement a complete stop on immigration, but rather to how immigration is positively managed by existing policy.

Worker migration

In .this way, for example, specific types of worker immigration, including skilled 'PMT', seasonal (e.g. associated with agricultural work), or temporary training-related immigration, could be more explicitly supported on the basis of sound and objective economic reasoning. Of course, this is not as easy during economic recession as it would be during a period of economic growth. However, in the longer term, a more positive approach in this respect might not prove to be any more difficult to sustain than the *status quo* – a *status quo* characterized by restrictions without absolute control, and by isolated or *ad hoc* immigration programmes which are not explained on the basis of a coherent strategy.[3]

In this context, lessons can be learnt from the approach of the traditional immigration countries. As observed by Findlay, 'Even during periods of recession Canada, the USA and Australia have held to their pro-immigration stances, maintaining the view that positive selective immigration is to do with nation building and future economic well-being.' Findlay argues – in the context of Britain – that 'politicians need to consider very carefully why their stance on immigration has not shifted in line with changes in the international migration system and why their view of immigration is so different from that of countries like Canada' (Findlay, 1993:10).

---

[3] It is interesting to note that in an opinion poll carried out in Spain in December 1992, the majority of respondents were in favour of the introduction of immigration quotas. Proposals for setting quotas for immigrant workers have been under consideration in Spain; and in Italy, the Ministries of Foreign Affairs, Economy, Employment and Social Security put forward an annual programme on migration quotas by an interministerial decree in January 1993. On 22 June 1993, the Italian government approved rules to formalize the status of seasonal worker. See *Migration News Sheet*, February 1993, April 1993, July 1993 and August 1993. Such measures are aimed at gaining better control over current levels of unregulated worker immigration.

A more positive stance on existing worker immigration depends on informed discourse about the economic effects of that immigration (see Chapters 1 and 3). This is a complex question, but the popular perception that immigration automatically results in an occupational displacement of indigenous workers, or the common confusion of the impacts of immigration with economic problems associated with more settled minority populations, can be challenged on the basis of existing research. An example of this is the linking of high unemployment among settled minority populations with the potential outcome of current or future immigration. This is, in fact, largely attributable to structural changes in those sectors of the labour market in which such populations are settled, or to discrimination against such populations within the labour market (see Findlay, 1993:2). Indeed, on balance, a great deal of immigration may be found to be economically beneficial. This includes non-worker categories, such as family immigration. All categories of immigrant may affect the economy, whether in terms of their participation in the labour market, as entrepreneurs, or as consumers. Yet, as Findlay observes, the economic dimensions of immigration are rarely considered directly by those moulding immigration policy (Findlay, 1993:1).[4]

Family migration
The principle supporting family immigration is less complex, less malleable, and, at least on the face of it, less open to question than arguments supporting 'economic' immigration. Thus, in these cases, one might expect more positive messages to emerge from policy-makers. A report on migration policy issued by the European Commission in 1991 explains that:

[4] Indeed, in the UK, there is a paucity of research into the economic impacts of immigration. Most recent research into the economic impacts of immigration in Western Europe has been carried out in Germany. See, for example, papers prepared for the seminar on 'The Economic and Social Impact of Migration' organized by the Institute for Public Policy Research and the Friedrich Ebert Foundation, London, March 1993.

all Member States have adopted restrictive provisions concerning permanent legal immigration for economic, social and hence political reasons. This reflects the discretionary powers retained by Member States with regard to economic migration ... [But] this principle has become less effective because it includes exceptions which have gradually come to overshadow the principle ... [These exceptions include] family reunification: given that a family unit living together remains one of the basic pillars of western societies, Member States permit the arrival of other members of the family (Commission of the European Communities, 1991:9–10).

However, the Commission notes that 'divergences affect practices from one Member State to another' and that the 'resultant exponential effects, together with certain abuses, call into question the extent of ... this traditional principle' (Commission of the European Communities, 1991:14).

Largely because of the period of significant family immigration which followed the halt on foreign labour recruitment in the early 1970s, family immigration is associated primarily with the consolidation of immigrant minority populations in Western Europe – at least in the public mind. This, again, reflects a confusion and clouding of categories. Family unity is a principle which stands apart from immigration, and is of potential importance to every citizen and every resident, particularly as personal contacts expand and intensify across national borders.[5] It could be explained and supported on this basis, as it is in the Canadian Immigration Act of 1978, which aims to 'facilitate reunion between Canadians / permanent residents and their relatives abroad' (quoted by Spencer, 1993:5).

---

[5] Note that in the United States, the General Accounting Office found that more than two-thirds of all visas issued for family migration were issued to the immediate families of native-born Americans. See Papademetriou, 1993:58.

Asylum

Similarly, as Chapter 4 has shown, asylum has become progressively divorced from its human rights and humanitarian context in public perceptions as 'abusive' applications have become confused with asylum applications in general. Asylum is thus increasingly seen as a cumbersome, expensive and unregulated channel of immigration, rather than as a policy grounded in fundamental principles of human rights and refugee protection. If the countries of Western Europe are to maintain a commitment to protecting refugees, they will have to remain at least partially open to asylum inflows (whether for durable asylum or temporary refuge). Thus, there is good reason for governments to work with human rights advocates and other non-governmental bodies to maintain and develop public understanding and acceptance of the principles supporting refugee protection, rather than play on public anxieties over immigration to gain support for restrictive measures. A demystification of the issue would provide a starting-point in this respect.

Settled minority populations

A shift in the tone of the policy debate could also contribute positively to an easing of tensions between majority and immigrant minority populations. Governments have shown a positive commitment to securing the successful integration of immigrant-minority populations, at least in principle. Yet they have also shown a tendency to react defensively to negative attitudes relating to immigrants and immigration among the public – not least in terms of the thrust of their immigration policies – rather than test their leadership role by attempting to challenge such attitudes head-on. As argued in earlier chapters, immigration policies based entirely on concepts of restriction and control have the effect of labelling immigration as a problem. Hence, a failure to stress the positive aspects of immigration might reinforce anti-immigrant sentiment and, as a result, exacerbate tension between majority and minority populations and thus hinder processes of immigrant integration. As noted in Chapter 2, the integration of immigrant minorities, and the development of 'multicultural' societies in Western Europe, are fragile processes which depend to a large extent on the messages conveyed to minority and majority populations by politicians and policy-makers, specifically in their stance on immigration and integration.

Of course, to argue for a more positive stance on particular categories of immigration is not to advocate that all the doors be opened. Indeed, a more positive approach to those categories of immigration which are allowed depends on a firm and consistent stance against those which are not, including unauthorized 'economic' immigration and 'abusive' asylum applications. However, there are good reasons for arguing that these defensive efforts ought not to colour the entire policy debate, and that restrictive control measures be formulated and explained in realistic terms. Western Europe is no longer in a position to decide whether or not it is a region of immigration, and thus a more constructive and forward-looking policy debate is only likely to emerge if efforts are made wherever possible to justify and explain the immigration which continues.[6]

Indeed, a further argument for more positive political efforts in the field may be found in their symbolic value, for immigration policy conveys important messages relating to public perceptions of society and its future. The perception of Western society as founded on concepts of openness, tolerance, respect for human rights and commitment to democracy and civic values – arguably essential for the future cohesion and stability of West European societies – is difficult to reconcile with immigration and refugee policies which convey messages of closure, isolation and intolerance of the outsider, and which erode basic civic or human rights principles such as family unity and protection for victims of persecution.

[6] Note a recent information campaign carried out by the Dutch government on the positive impacts of immigration.

The longer term

Because migration is a highly complex process, and because current migration pressures are severe, there are no 'quick fixes' at policy-makers' disposal. Despite the introduction of stricter policies, immigration into Western Europe has continued to increase since the early 1980s. The total inflow of foreigners into Western Europe in 1991 has been estimated at around 1.5 million (Salt et al., 1993). Thus, might a policy regime which openly incorporates the existence and persistence of immigration prove not only more politically viable, but also more effective in the longer term?

In Western Europe, the end of the Cold War and the acceleration of the EC integration process have brought about new pressures and a new impetus for more dynamic policy development in all sorts of spheres. In migration policy, this is reflected in the increasing concern with the root causes of migration, in the development of wider regional structures of cooperation, and in some new and positive – albeit limited – immigration initiatives, such as temporary training-related immigration programmes, such as those set up between Germany and the Visegrad states (see Hofler, 1992). In refugee policy, as discussed in Chapter 4, this impetus is reflected in a new emphasis on concepts of prevention and durable resolution in the countries and regions of origin.

Yet, as noted in earlier chapters, attachment to the old order in migration affairs is strong. The economic and political uncertainty of the early 1990s, and the intractability of problems associated with migration have frustrated any substantive progress towards the development of a more comprehensive and positive policy regime. Attention is still focused almost exclusively on migration problems in the receiving states of Western Europe, and on short-term protective measures. This limits new policy initiatives, including those aimed at cooperation with the countries of Eastern/ Central Europe and the southern Mediterranean, and proposals for tackling the root causes of migration.

The importance of widening the scope of migration policy can be illustrated by reference to the potentially perverse implications of recent short-cut policy initiatives. For instance, efforts to create a migration-control 'buffer zone' around Western Europe – including a number of bilateral or regional instruments involving cooperation on the part of the East/Central European states, as discussed in Chapter 3 – may prove effective in terms of short-term control. They will facilitate expulsions, and impel 'transit' states to develop their own immigration regulations to comply with the entry conditions of West European states (O'Keefe, 1993:195). Yet in the longer term these efforts could have adverse political effects. First, the introduction of strict border controls is politically difficult for the Central/East European states, as it carries with it the echoes of the pre-1989 restrictions on movement. Indeed, tensions are already manifest between the Czech Republic and Slovakia over recent moves on the part of the Czech government to control and restrict movement across the country's eastern border.

Second, barriers to movement into Western Europe, coupled with the deflection of flows back from there, could impose substantial strains on the fragile institutional, political, economic and social structures of the Central/East European states, despite promises of financial assistance to ease the tensions. As asserted in the statement of the Hungarian delegation at a recent CSCE seminar on migration in Europe, 'tens and tens of thousands of refugees have come to Hungary. We have come to the limits of our economic possibilities, to the limits of our capabilities to shelter more refugees.'[7] There is a contradiction operating here between the short-term concern to restrict immigration, and the longer-term aim to assist the difficult and fragile processes of economic, political and social reform in the former Eastern bloc countries.

This tension is manifest in current developments in asylum policy. As discussed in Chapter 4, the recent response of the West European states to increasing numbers of asylum applications has been to propose or introduce policies which stress their negative, as opposed to positive, responsibilities *vis-à-vis* asylum-seekers. Of particular relevance in this context is the 1993 Resolution reached

[7] Conference on Security and Cooperation in Europe: Human Dimension Seminar on Migration, including Refugees and Displaced Persons, Warsaw, April 1993.

by EC immigration ministers on 'third host countries' (see Chapter 4), which seeks to place responsibility for processing claims and providing refugee protection on the 'buffer states' through which asylum-seekers may travel to seek asylum in the West. While there may be immediate political and pragmatic justifications for this approach, it discounts the great importance of standard-setting. Asylum is still a fragile institution in the former Eastern bloc states. If Western Europe is seen to be closing its doors to asylum-seekers, who is to say that the countries of Eastern/Central Europe should not do the same? Moreover, if West European states are to uphold protection from persecution and violence as a fundamental principle – not least for the sake of preventive efforts in the field – then it is imperative that they themselves demonstrate a full and positive commitment to the principle of refugee protection. As argued by Loescher, 'restrictive measures taken unilaterally by Western states serve not to solve the problem but pass it on to some other country to resolve, thus contributing to interstate tensions, protectionism, and a breakdown in the international refugee regime' (Loescher, 1992a:3).

Towards a regional view

These examples point to a number of shortcomings in the evolving regime of refugee and migration policy in Western Europe. These derive principally from a failure to think regionally, to think long-term, and to step back and reach a reasoned and balanced evaluation of mutual capacities and responsibilities *vis-à-vis* migration in the new Europe.

The member states of the European Community are, of course, as Chapter 3 has shown, thinking more regionally as concerns the integration and coordination of policy and the balancing of interests within the Community itself. Yet so far this has not been translated into an effective, equitable and sustainable cooperative regime at the trans-European or wider level (including, for example, the Southern Mediterranean states). This is indicated by recent developments in asylum policy, which reflect an assumption that while the countries of Western Europe cannot cope with current levels of asylum applications, poorer and less stable countries can. Recent cooperative initiatives represent, first and foremost, efforts to expand the West European control regime eastwards and southwards. Beyond this there is a great deal of multilateral activity, but it is so far extremely muddled and confused.

A more effective regional regime will only emerge on the basis of a clear and realistic assessment of both external and internal pressures, capacities, responsibilities and needs. Such a regime will depend on the political will of the states concerned to carry through proposals which may frequently appear politically risky or unpopular. For this will to develop, there has to be an appreciation of how a more equitable and forward-looking regime will ultimately benefit every country involved. Because it is unrealistic to expect migration to be halted, the greatest benefit would probably be the introduction of a sense of management and order into the process. This might enable governments better to capitalize on the benefits, and minimize the most disruptive effects of future migration.

A more positive regime might or might not result in actual increases in migration into Western Europe. However, it would almost certainly require a willingness on the part of governments to take responsibility for, or be open to accepting, greater numbers than has been the case in the past – whether it be in terms of positive immigration quotas (as operated in Canada, Australia and the United States), or simply in terms of maintaining a positive commitment to keeping 'windows' (Purcell, 1993) open for particular categories of immigration. It would also require a high degree of flexibility, enabling policies to be adapted to current realities and changing circumstances. Although difficult, such a regime would be politically viable, for the aim would not necessarily be to promote migration, but rather to promote greater order within it. While unlikely to provide a mechanism for perfect control, it could offer a useful instrument through which both sending and receiving states could articulate migration priorities and preferences

(Papademetriou, 1993). It could also inject a greater degree of predictability and planning into a process which, at present, is in danger of becoming increasingly unmanageable. Among other things, it might help prevent migration flows being deflected from one immigration channel into another as a result of restrictive policies; for example, potential labour flows into asylum channels, or potential asylum flows into undocumented channels (see Chapter 3).

A more forward-looking regime would also require more positive and concerted forms of cooperation at the regional or international level, in order for the interests and problems of sending or 'transit' states to be taken more fully into account in the strategies pursued by the West European states. At a pragmatic level, this might include an expansion of training-related temporary migration programmes, information programmes in the countries of origin, and more regulated return and reintegration programmes for rejected asylum-seekers and illegal migrants.

In terms of a broader policy framework, this would have to involve a closer integration of migration policy with a range of wider national, foreign and regional policies, including those related to regional human resource development. These include labour market policies, trade, aid, debt relief, conflict prevention and conflict resolution, the promotion of liberal society and respect for human rights, both at home and abroad. Recognition of a need for wider policy integration of this kind is reflected in the EC Declaration on the Principles Governing External Aspects of Migration Policy, issued in December 1992 (see Chapter 3). However, the assumption of this Declaration is that, on the basis of tackling the root causes, migration can be substantially reduced or even stopped. Because of the scale and complexity of the problems to be tackled in this context, because of other competing interests which will inevitably affect such policies, and because of the unpredictable nature of migration itself, this is an unrealistic expectation – at least in the short to medium term – and thus cannot form a good basis for policy. To formulate policy proposals on the basis of unrealistic expectations might, at best, encourage fire-fighting responses, or, at worst, result in no action being taken at all. What is desirable is that governments think more about the potential longer-term migration effects of their domestic and foreign policies (in the context of trade policies, for example); and about the potential economic, political and social effects of the migration policies they pursue – for example, the potential for political tensions in situations of conflict to be exacerbated if obstacles are put in the way of refugees' flight. In this way, both migration and other domestic and foreign policies might at least begin to shape migration in the most beneficial way for the future stability of the European continent. Such thinking will be most productive if it is developed openly, in dialogue with the various interests affected by migration, and also with migrants themselves.

Within the borders of a state, mobility is generally seen as a normal part of life, and it is recognized that people move for a variety of reasons and in a variety of contexts – to take up jobs, to find a more desirable place to live, to leave or join family members, or to receive education. Indeed, free movement within a state is generally accepted to be one of the fundamental liberties of citizens.[8] However, because we live in a world divided into states, movement across state borders is generally seen as an anomaly – an exception to the rule, and an exception over which the state, rather than the individual, has ultimate control.

Yet, in the modern world, international migration can no longer be seen as such an anomaly, nor can it be assumed that states have ultimate control over the process. It is a global phenomenon which affects every continent and virtually every country of the world. The traditional frontiers of the nation-state have been significantly weakened by a range of transnational and global economic, political, social and cultural forces, including migration. At a time of

[8] Note Article 13 of the Universal Declaration of Human Rights, which states that 'Everyone has the right to freedom of movement and residence within the borders of each state.' Note also that free movement within the European Community is seen as a fundamental component of EC citizenship.

considerable political and economic upheaval, there is a temptation to turn back to old certainties, and to the security of old frontiers. However, the old frontiers have become porous; the sense of security they bring is illusory. A new European order carries as its consequence an erosion of barriers. A commitment to a new Europe means a commitment to the challenges and opportunities of a new kind of national frontier.

References

Ad Hoc Group on Immigration (1991), 'Report from the Ministers Responsible for Immigration to the European Council Meeting in Maastricht on Immigration and Asylum Policy' (Work Programme), SN 4038/91 (WGI 930).

Ad Hoc Group on Immigration (1992), 'Conclusions of the Meeting of the Ministers Responsible for Immigration', (10518/92 [Presse 230]), Press Release, London, 30 November 1992.

Ad Hoc Group on Immigration (1993), 'Conclusions of the Meeting of Ministers Responsible for Immigration', Copenhagen, 2 June 1993.

Amnesty International (1991), 'Europe: Human Rights and the Need for a Fair Asylum Policy' (AI INDEX: EUR 01/03/91), London.

Amnesty International (1992), 'Europe: Harmonization of Asylum Policy: accelerated procedures for "manifestly unfounded" asylum claims and the "safe country" concept', paper issued by the Amnesty International EC Project, Brussels.

Baubock, R. (1992), 'Immigration and the Boundaries of Citizenship', Monographs in Ethnic Relations 4, Warwick, Centre for Research in Ethnic Relations.

Berlin Working Party (1993), 'Draft Recommendation', drawn up for the Budapest Intergovernmental Conference to Prevent Uncontrolled Migration, Budapest, February 1993.

Böhning, W.R. (1981), 'Elements of a Theory of International Economic Migration to Industrial Nation States', in M.M. Kritz, C.B. Keely and S.M. Tomasi, eds., *Global Trends in International Migration. Theory and Research on International Population Movements*, New York, Center for Migration Studies (third printing, 1983).

Brochmann, G. (1992), 'Control at What Cost?', paper prepared for the workshop on 'Migration into Western Europe: What Way Forward?', Royal Institute of International Affairs, London, November 1992.

Castles, S., Booth, H. and Wallace, T. (1984), *Here For Good: Western Europe's New Ethnic Minorities*, London, Pluto Press.

Castles, S. and Kosack, G. (1973), *Immigrant Workers and Class Structure in Western Europe*, Oxford, Oxford University Press.

Coleman, D.A. (1992), 'Does Europe Need Immigrants? Population and Work Force Projections', *International Migration Review*, vol. 26, no. 2.

Coles, G. (1989), 'Approaching the Refugee Problem Today', in G. Loescher and L. Monahan, eds., *Refugees and International Relations*, New York, Oxford University Press.

Coles, G. (1992), 'Changing Perspectives of Refugee Law and Policy' in V. Gowlland and K. Samson, eds, *Problems and Prospects of Refugee Law*, Geneva, The Graduate Institute of International Studies.

Collinson, S. (1993), *Europe and International Migration*, London, Pinter Publishers for the Royal Institute of International Affairs.

Collinson, S., Miall, H. and Michalski, A. (1993), *A Wider European Union? Integration and Cooperation in the New Europe*, RIIA Discussion Paper No. 48, London, Royal Institute of International Affairs.

Commission for the Study of International Migration and Cooperative Economic Development (1990), *Unauthorised Migration: An Economic Development Response*, Report of the Commission, submitted to the White House, the United States Senate and the United States House of Representatives, Washington DC, July 1990.

Commission of the European Communities (1990), 'Policies on Immigration and the Social Integration of Migrants in the European Community', Experts' report drawn up on behalf of the Commission of the European Communities, Brussels, Commission of the European Communities.

Commission of the European Communities (1991), 'Commission Communication to the Council and European Parliament on Immigration' (SEC(91) 1855 final), Brussels, Commission of the European Communities.

Council of Europe (1991), 'Community and Ethnic Relations in Europe', Final report of the Community Relations Project of the Council of Europe, (MG-CR (91) 1 final E), Strasbourg, Council of Europe.

Danish Refugee Council and The Danish Center of Human Rights (1991), *The Effects of Carrier Sanctions on the Asylum System*, Copenhagen, Danish Refugee Council.

Douglas, M. (1975), *Implicit Meanings: Essays in Anthropology*, London, Melbourne, Boston and Henley, Routledge & Kegan Paul.

Emmerij, Louis (1991), 'The International Situation, Economic Development and Employment', paper presented at the OECD International Conference on Migration, Rome, March 1991.

European Communities (1990), *Bulletin of the European Communities*, no. 6–1990, Brussels, EC.

European Council (1992), 'Declaration on Principles Governing External Aspects of Migration Policy', in the Conclusions of the Presidency (SN 456/1/92 REV 1), Edinburgh, 12 December 1992.

Federal Minister of the Interior (1991), 'Survey of the Policy and Law Regarding Aliens in the Federal Republic of Germany', The Federal Minister of the Interior (V II 1 - 937 020/15 [Translation]), Bonn, Federal Ministry of the Interior.

Findlay, A. (1993), 'The Economic Impact of Immigration to the United Kingdom: Trends and Policy Implications', paper prepared for the seminar on The Economic and Social Impact of Migration organized by the Institute for Public Policy Research and the Friedrich Ebert Foundation, London, March 1993.

Gaeremynck, J. (1993), 'Les croyances religieuses à l'école: à propos de la décision récente du Conseil d'Etat sur le port du foulard', *Migrations Societé* 5/25.

Garcia, S. (1992), *Europe's Fragmented Identities and the Frontiers of Citizenship*, RIIA Discussion Paper No. 45, London, Royal Institute of International Affairs.

Gellner, E. (1964), *Thought and Change*, London, Weidenfeld & Nicolson.

Gellner, E. (1983), *Nations and Nationalism*, Oxford, Blackwell.

Gibney, Mark, ed. (1988), *Open Borders? Closed Societies? The Ethical and Political Issues*, Contributions in Political Science no. 226, Westport, Connecticut, Greenwood Press.

Gieseck, A., Heilemann, U. and Dietrich von Loeffelholz, H. (1993), 'Economic and Social Implications of Migration into the Federal Republic of Germany', RWI-Papiere No. 35, Essen, Rheinisch-Westfälisches Institut für Wirtschaftsforschung.

Grahl-Madsen, A. (1966, 1972), *The Status of Refugees in International Law*, Leyden, A.W. Sijthoff.

Guild, E. (1992), *Protecting Migrants' Rights: Application of EC Agreements with Third Countries*, CCME Briefing Paper no. 10, Brussels, Churches Committee for Migrants in Europe.

Habermas, J. (1991), 'Citizenship and National Identity: Some Reflections on the Future of Europe', paper presented at the conference 'Identité et Différences dans l'Europe Démocratique', Louvain-La-Neuve.

Hammar, T. (1990), *Democracy and the Nation-state: Aliens, Denizens, and Citizens in a World of International Migration*, Aldershot, Avebury (Gower Publishing).

Hathaway, J. (1991), *The Law of Refugee Status*, Vancouver, Butterworths Canada Ltd.

Hofler, L. (1992), 'Migration Programmes of the Federal Republic of Germany Aimed at the Training and Short-term Employment of Workers Originating from Developing Countries or Countries of Central or Eastern Europe', paper delivered at the 10th International Organization for Migration Seminar on Migration and Development, Geneva, September 1992.

Home Office (1990), Policy Statement on the Criteria for Ethnic Minority Grants, London, Home Office.

Isajiw, W. (1975), 'Immigration and Multiculturalism – Old and New Approaches', paper prepared for the conference on Multiculturalism and Third World Immigrants in Canada, University of Alberta.

Jaeger, G. (1993), 'The Recent Concept and Policy of Preventive Protection', in *Refugee Participation Network* no. 14.

Knight, F. (1921), *Risk, Uncertainty and Profit*, Boston, Houghton Mifflin.

Kritz, M.M., Keely, C.B. and Tomasi, S.M., eds. (1981), *Global Trends in International Migration. Theory and Research on International Population Movements*, New York, Center for Migration Studies (third printing, 1983).

Kubat, Daniel, ed. (1993), *The Politics of Migration Policies. Settlement and Integration: The First World into the 1990s*, (second edition), New York, Center for Migration Studies.

Layton-Henry, Z. (1990), *The Political Rights of Migrant Workers in Western Europe*, Sage Modern Politics Series 25, London, Sage Publications.

Livi-Bacci, M. (1991), 'South – North Migration: A Comparative Approach to North American and European Experiences', paper presented to the OECD International Conference on Migration, Rome, March 1991.

Loescher, G., ed. (1992a), *Refugees and the Asylum Dilemma in the West*, Pennsylvania, The Pennsylvania State University Press (first published as a special issue of *Journal of Policy History* 4/1).

Loescher, G. (1992b), *Refugee Movements and International Security*, Adelphi Paper 268, London, Brassey's for the International Institute for Strategic Studies.

Loescher, G. and Scanlan, J. (1986), *Calculated Kindness: Refugees and America's Half-Open Door*, New York and London, The Free Press and Macmillan.

Martin, D. A. (1988), 'The New Asylum Seekers', in D. A. Martin, ed., *The New Asylum Seekers: Refugee Law in the 1980s* (Ninth Sohol Colloquium on International Law, University of Virginia, 1986), International Studies in Human Rights 10, Dordrecht, Martinus Nijhoff Publishers.

Meijers, H. et al. (1991), *Schengen. Internationalisation of Central Chapters of the Law on Aliens, Refugees, Privacy, Security and the Police*, W.E.J. Tjeenk Willink - Kluwer Law and Taxation, Netherlands.

Migration News Sheet, various issues, Brussels, European Information Network.

Miles, R. and Pluzacklea, A. (1977), 'Class, race, ethnicity and political action', *Political Studies*, vol. 25, no. 4.

Netherlands Scientific Council for Government Policy (1990), 'Immigrant Policy: Summary of the 36th Report', Reports to the Government 36, The Hague.

Newland, K. (1993a), 'Ethnic Conflict and Refugees', *Survival* 35/1.

Newland, K. (1993b), 'Emergency Population Displacements', paper prepared for the conference on The Security Dimensions of International Migration in Europe, organized by the Center for Strategic and International Studies (Washington DC), Sicily, April 1993.

Nielsen, J.S. (1992), *Muslims in Western Europe*, Islamic Surveys 20, Edinburgh, Edinburgh University Press.

OECD (various dates), *Continuous Reporting System on Migration (SOPEMI)*, Paris, OECD.

Office of Population Censuses and Surveys (1993), *International Migration 1991. United Kingdom: England and Wales*, Series MN no. 18, London, HMSO (Government Statistical Office).

Ogata, S. (1992), 'Refugees: A Comprehensive European Strategy', statement made at the Peace Palace, The Hague, 24 November.

Ogata, S. (1993a), 'Challenge to the United Nations: A Humanitarian Perspective', statement delivered at the Centre for the Study of Global Governance, London School of Economics, 4 May.

Ogata, S. (1993b), 'Refugees: Lessons from the Past', Richard Storry Lecture delivered at St Antony's College, Oxford, 5 May.

O'Keefe, D. (1993), 'The Schengen Convention: A Suitable Model for European Integration?', in *Yearbook of European Law 1993.*

Owers, Anne (1993), 'The Age of Internal Controls?', in Sarah Spencer, ed., *Immigration and Refugees: New Directions for Britain*, London, Rivers Oram/IPPR, forthcoming October.

Papademetriou, Demetrios G. (1993), 'At the Precipice? Some Thoughts about Where Europe is with Regard to Migration, How it Got There, and What it Might Do About It', paper prepared for the conference on The Security Dimensions of International Migration in Europe, organized by the Center for Strategic and International Studies (Washington DC), Sicily, April 1993.

Piore, M. (1979), *Birds of Passage: Migrant Labour and Industrial Societies*, Cambridge, Cambridge University Press.

Plender, R. (1988), *International Migration Law*, revised 2nd edn, Dordrecht, Nijhoff.

Purcell, J. (1993), 'Towards a Comprehensive Approach to the Migration Challenge of the 1990s', lecture delivered at the Royal Institute of International Affairs, London, May 1993.

Rex, J. (1985), 'The Concept of a Multi-Cultural Society', Occasional Papers in Ethnic Relations 3, Warwick, Centre for Research in Ethnic Relations.

Rex, J., Joly, D. and Wilpert, C., eds. (1987), *Immigrant Associations in Europe*, Aldershot and Vermont, Gower Publishing for the European Science Foundation.

Rosoli, G. (1993), 'Italy: Emergent Immigration Policy', in D. Kubat, ed., *The Politics of Migration Policies. Settlement and Integration: the First World into the 1990s* (Second Edition), New York, Center for Migration Studies.

Rudge, P. (1992), 'The Asylum Dilemma – Crisis in the Modern World: A European Perspective', in G. Loescher, ed., *Refugees and the Asylum Dilemma in the West*, Pennsylvania, The Pennsylvania State

University Press (first published as a special issue of *Journal of Policy History* 4/1).

Salt, John (1991), 'Current and Future International Migration Trends Affecting Europe', paper prepared for the Fourth Conference of European Ministers Responsible for Migration Affairs, Luxembourg, September 1991 (MMG-4 (91) 1 E), Strasbourg, Council of Europe.

Salt, John (1993), 'The Future of International Labor Migration', paper prepared for the seminar on The Economic and Social Impact of Migration organized by the Institute for Public Policy Research (London) and the Friedrich Ebert Foundation (Bonn), London, March 1993 (to be published in *International Migration Review*, 1993).

Salt, J., Singleton, A. and Hogarth, J. (1993), *Contemporary International Migration in Europe*, forthcoming.

Schmitter Heisler, B. (1992), 'The Future of Immigrant Incorporation: Which Models? Which Concepts?', *International Migration Review* 26/2.

Schuck, P. (1985), 'Immigration Law and the Problem of Community', in N. Glazer (ed.), *Clamor at the Gates*, San Francisco, ICS Press.

Shacknove, A. (1985), 'Who is a Refugee?', *Ethics* 95.

Simon, J. (1993), 'The Economic Effects of Immigration', *European Review* 1/1.

Singer, P. and Singer, R. (1988), 'The Ethics of Refugee Policy', in Gibney, M., ed., *Open Borders? Closed Societies? The Ethical and Political Issues*, Contributions in Political Science no. 226, Westport, CT, Greenwood Press.

Skran, C. (1992), 'The International Refugee Regime: The Historical and Contemporary Context of International Responses to Asylum Problems', in G. Loescher, ed., *Refugees and the Asylum Dilemma in the West*.

Smith, A. (1991), *National Identity*, London, Penguin Books.

Smith, A. (1992), 'National Identity and the Idea of European Unity', *International Affairs* 28/1.

Spencer, S. (1993), 'The Social and Political Objectives of Immigration Policy', paper prepared for the seminar on The Economic and Social Impact of Migration organized by the Institute for Public Policy Research and the Friedrich Ebert Foundation, London, March 1993.

Stenberg, G. (1989), *Non-Expulsion and Non-Refoulement: the Prohibition against Removal of Refugees with Special Reference to Articles 32 and 33 of the 1951 Convention Relating to the Status of Refugees* (Studies in International Law), Uppsala, Iustus Förlag.

Straubhaar, T. and Zimmerman, K. (1992), *Towards a European Migration Policy*, CEPR Discussion Paper No. 641, London, Centre for Economic Policy Research.

UNHCR (1988), *Handbook on Procedures and Criteria for Determining Refugee Status under the 1951 Convention and the 1967 Protocol Relating to the Status of Refugees* (HCR /IP / Eng. Rev. 1), Geneva, UNHCR.

UNHCR (1992a), 'Note on International Protection' (A./AC.96/799), Geneva, UNHCR.

UNHCR (1992b), 'General Conclusion on International Protection' (A/AC.96/802), Geneva, UNHCR.

UNHCR (1993), 'Survey of the Implementation of Temporary Protection', paper prepared for the Comprehensive Response to the Humanitarian Crisis in the Former Yugoslavia (30 April 1993), Geneva, UNHCR.

United Nations (1985), *International Cooperation to Avert New Flows of Refugees*, Group of Experts' Report of 13 May 1985 (UN.A/41/324), New York, United Nations.

US Committee for Refugees (1993), *World Refugee Survey 1993*, Washington DC, American Council for Nationalities Service.

Van Praag, C.S. (1986), 'Minderheden voor en na de nota' (Minorities before and after the Policy Document), *Migrantenstudies* 2/4.

Walzer, M. (1983), *Spheres of Justice*, New York, Basic Books.

Weiner, M. (1993), 'Security, Stability and International Migration', *International Security* 17/3.

Widgren, J. (1991), 'The Management of Mass Migration in a European Context', lecture delivered at the Royal Institute of International Affairs, London, March 1991.

Widgren, Jonas (1993), 'The Need for a New Multilateral Order to Prevent Mass Movements from Becoming a Security Threat in Europe', paper prepared for the conference on The Security Dimensions of International Migration in Europe, organized by the Center for Strategic and International Studies (Washington DC), Sicily, April 1993.

Zolberg, A. (1981), 'International Migrations in Political Perspective', in M.M. Kritz, C.B. Keely and S.M. Tomasi, eds., *Global Trends in International Migration. Theory and Research on International Population Movements*, New York, Center for Migration Studies (third printing, 1983).

Zolberg, A., Suhrke, A., and Aguayo, S. (1989), *Escape from Violence. Conflict and the Refugee Crisis in the Developing World*, New York and Oxford, Oxford University Press.

Recommendations of the Wyndham Place Trust

The recommendations of the Wyndham Place Trust are as follows. In the short term five steps are recommended:

1. There should be greater *openness* in the formulation of policy and in its implementation, both at national and at European levels.
2. *The migration of workers* should be seen to be as much a contribution to economic well-being as a threat to the indigenous labour force.
3. *Migration for purposes of family reunification* should be regarded as positive, given that the right of families to live together is a basic value of European societies.
4. *The granting of asylum* to refugees is a consequence of the basic commitment of European countries to the protection of human rights and should be reaffirmed.
5. Governments should secure for *settled minority populations* the rights accorded to all citizens of their states.

The following further recommendations are made for action in the longer term:

6. European countries should reinforce their help to countries of emigration in order to reduce the economic, social and political root causes of emigration.
7. The standard of protection and support afforded to refugees seeking asylum should be raised so as to give them economic independence.

114

8. Issues of migration should progressively be resolved in a European rather than a bilateral context in order to harmonize, as far as possible, the respective needs and interests of sending, transit and receiving states.

9. Governments should give consideration to the potential longer-term effects of their migration policies on their own countries and on the sending ones. Such consideration should be undertaken in consultation with migrant interests.

Appendix: Stocks of foreign population by nationality: major recruitment countries and major immigrant groups in the early 1980s and 1990 (in thousands)

	Belgium		France		Germany		Netherlands		UK		Switzerland	
Nationality	1981	1990	1982	1990	1980	1990	1980	1990	1984	1990	1980	1990
Italy	277	241	340	254	618	548	21	17	83	75	421	379
Ireland	1	2	—	—	—	—	—	—	491	638	—	—
Spain	58	52	327	216	180	135	23	17	25	24	97	116
Portugal	11	17	767	646	112	85	9	8	10[a]	21	11	86
Greece	21	21	—	—	298	315	4	5	—	—	9	8
Turkey	66	85	122	202	1462	1675	139	204	—	—	38	64
former Yugoslavia	6	6	63	52	632	653	14	14	—	—	44	141
Algeria	11	11	805	620	5[b]	7	—	—	—	—	—	—
Morocco	110	142	441	585	36	66	83	157	—	—	—	—
Tunisia	7	6	191	208	23	26	2	3	—	—	—	—
Poland	—	—	65	46	88[c]	241	—	—	—	—	—	5
New C'wealth & E/W Africa	—	—	—	—	—	—	—	—	442	394	—	—
Other countries	318	322	593	780	999	1491	226	267	550	723	273	301
Total	886	905	3714	3609	4453	5242	521	692	1601	1875	893	1100
of which EEC	594	550	1595	1309	1494[d]	1325[e]	171	168	701[f]	889	701	760

[a]Less than 10,000; [b]Figure for 1983; [c]Figure for 1982; [d]Figure for 1983; [e]Figure for 1989; [f]Figure for 1983

Source: SOPEMI (OECD Continuous Reporting System on Migration), *Trends in International Migration*, OECD, Paris, 1992.